OVERCOMING
THE FORCES OF
LIFE

LIBERATION
HOUR MESSAGES
VOL. 1

SEKUDO MICHAEL AJIBOYE

Appreciation

All gratitude goes to God who is the Giver of wisdom and understanding, for the inspiration given to put this together and for this piece to be a blessing to others. My appreciation goes to my lovely wife and my children for sacrificing their time and comfort at the moment of working on this book.

I wish to sincerely appreciate the impacts of my spiritual fathers: Bishop David Oyedepo and Bishop David Abioye, my mentors, seniors, leaders, friends, well wishers and colleagues in the work of the ministry for the inspiration, words of encouragement and support received towards this publication.

I will not forget to acknowledge the effort of my graphic designer Daniel Agboje, who typed, compiled and designed the content of this book. My sincere appreciation goes to the CEO of MIKETOJANE PRINTING AND PUBLISHING LIMITED for editing, professional packaging and publishing of the book.

This piece is the original work of the author. No part of this book is permitted to be reproduced or used for publication, intellectual discuss, without permission and reference to the author of this book.

Type Setting/Compilation:
Daniel Agboje
Tel: 07035730526, 08067268410
Email: dan4exploit@gmail.com
Website: idealtech.com.ng
Port Harcourt, Nigeria.

Publisher : Miketojane Ltd.
Tel: 08033688772, 08057314120
Email : miketojane.info@gmail.com

TABLE OF CONTENT

INTRODUCTION

Inspirations are products of divine revelations delivered by the Spirit of God to man; documented to impact and transform others. This publication   is a product of such Revelational experience. Be blessed as you go through this piece of work.

SEKUDO MICHAEL AJIBOYE
@michaelajiboye4@gmail.com
@msekudo(Twitter)
michaelajiboyesekudo(Instagram)
www.d-blossomsupernaturalhighways.org.ng

CHAPTER ONE
OVERCOMING THE FORCES OF LIFE

Life is governed by supernatural forces. The manifestation of either positive or negative forces is also governed by supernatural powers, which birth positive or negative experiences in our lives. In this chapter, we shall be looking at what keeps a man perpetually on one spots or at best on a slow motion experience. These forces of life operate in various dimensions. To start with, we shall be looking at the "forces in our family foundation".

WHAT ARE THE FORCES IN OUR FAMILY FOUNDATION?

They are the negative experiences in our lives as a result of the covenants our parents entered into, which have translated into a generational battle. Also, these forces can be triggered by the iniquities of our parents. These negative experiences have become a pattern in most families running through the blood line, as though it is a normal way of life. For instance every male child dies at fifty (50)years of age; every female child never marries honourably; every member of the family struggles to succeed; reoccurrences of spiritual husbands and wives; association with marine spirits; male children never give birth to male babies; unknown sources of premature death, etc. Hence, the factors that are responsible for these negative experience and solution to each of them shall be presented in a logical manner.

FORCES IN OUR FAMILY FOUNDATION.
A: THE INIQUITIES OF OUR FATHERS.

(Lamentation 5:7)
" our fathers have sinned and are no more, but we borne their iniquities.

WHAT ARE THE CONSEQUENCES OF THE INIQUITIES OF OUR FATHERS

(Lam. 5:1-22)
Remember, O LORD, what is come upon us: consider, and behold our reproach. Our inheritance is turned to strangers, our houses to aliens. We are orphans and fatherless, our mothers are as widows. We have drunken our water for money; our wood is sold unto us. Our necks are under persecution: we labour, and have no rest. We have given the hand to the Egyptians, and to the Assyrians, to be satisfied with bread. Our fathers have sinned, and are not; and we have borne their iniquities. Servants have ruled over us: there is none that doth deliver us out of their hand. We gat our bread with the peril of our lives because of the sword of the wilderness. Our skin was black like an oven because of the terrible famine. They ravished the women in Zion, and the maids in the cities of Judah. Princes are hanged up by their hand: the faces of elders were not honoured. They took the young men to grind, and the children fell under the wood. The elders have ceased from the gate, the young men from their musick. The joy of our heart is ceased; our dance is turned into mourning. The crown is fallen from our head: woe unto us, that we have sinned! For this our heart is faint; for these things our eyes are dim. Because of the mountain of Zion, which is desolate, the foxes walk upon it. Thou, O LORD, remainest for ever; thy throne from generation to generation. Wherefore dost thou forget us for ever, and forsake us so long time? Turn thou us unto thee, O LORD, and we shall be turned; renew our days as of old. But thou hast utterly rejected us; thou art very wroth against us.

CONSEQUENCES OF THE INIQUITIES OF OUR FATHERS.
- You suffer for what you didn't know anything about.
- It keeps you on one spot.
- You go through re-occurrence of negative life situations, sometimes the same or multiple experiences.

- It multiplies sorrow in the life of an individual.
- It leads to spiritual blindness. **(John 44:17-18.)**

And the residue thereof he maketh a god, even his graven image: he falleth down unto it, and worshippeth it, and prayeth unto it, and saith, Deliver me; for thou art my god. They have not known nor understood: for he hath shut their eyes, that they cannot see; and their hearts, that they cannot understand.

HOW TO BE DELIVERED:

- **You renounce vehemently the forces in your foundation.**

(2 Chronicle 25:1-4.) *Amaziah was twenty and five years old when he began to reign, and he reigned twenty and nine years in Jerusalem. And his mother's name was Jehoaddan of Jerusalem. And he did that which was right in the sight of the LORD, but not with a perfect heart. Now it came to pass, when the kingdom was established to him, that he slew his servants that had killed the king his father. But he slew not their children, but did as it is written in the law in the book of Moses, where the LORD commanded, saying, The fathers shall not die for the children, neither shall the children die for the fathers, but every man shall die for his own sin.*

- **Cry unto God for supernatural intervention.**

(Psalm.79:11) *Let the sighing of the prisoner come before thee; according to the greatness of thy power preserve thou those that are appointed to die;*

- **Enforce your deliverance by the blood of Jesus.**

(Zechariah 9:11) *as for thee also, by the blood of thy covenant I have sent forth thy prisoners out of the pit wherein no water is.*

B: GENERATIONAL BATTLE OF THE FIRST BORN

1. Abraham's first child in the flesh, ISHMAEL did not receive the It was given to ISAAC.

Gen. 17:20 *And as for Ishmael, I have heard thee: Behold, I have blessed him, and will make him fruitful, and will multiply him exceedingly; twelve princes shall he beget, and I will make him a great nation.,*

Gen. 21:8-22. *And the child grew, and was weaned: and Abraham made a great feast the same day that Isaac was weaned: And Sarah saw the son of Hagar the Egyptian, which she had born unto Abraham, mocking. Wherefore she said unto Abraham, Cast out this bondwoman and her son: for the son of this bondwoman shall not be heir with my son, even with Isaac. And the thing was very grievous in Abraham's sight because of his son. And God said unto Abraham, Let it not be grievous in thy sight because of the lad, and because of thy bondwoman; in all that Sarah hath said unto thee, hearken unto her voice; for in Isaac shall thy seed be called. And also of the son of the bondwoman will I make a nation, because he is thy seed. And Abraham rose up early in the morning, and took bread, and a bottle of water, and gave it unto Hagar, putting it on her shoulder, and the child, and sent her away: and she departed, and wandered in the wilderness of Beer-sheba. And the water was spent in the bottle, and she cast the child under one of the shrubs. And she went, and sat her down over against him a good way off, as it were a bowshot: for she said, Let me not see the death of the child. And she sat over against him, and lift up her voice, and wept. And God heard the voice of the lad; and the angel of God called Hagar out of heaven, and said unto her, What aileth thee, Hagar? fear not; for God hath heard the voice of the lad where he is.: Arise, lift up the lad, and hold him in thine hand; for I will make him a great nation. And God opened her eyes, and she saw a well of water; and she went, and filled the bottle with water, and gave the lad drink. And God was with the lad; and he grew, and dwelt in the wilderness, and became an archer. And he dwelt in the wilderness of Paran: and his mother took him a wife out of the land of Egypt. And it came to pass at that time, that Abimelech and Phichol the chief captain of his host spake unto Abraham, saying, God is with thee in all that thou doest:*

2.	Isaac's first child ESAU, didn't receive the inheritance.	It was given to JACOB.

Gen. 25:21-23 *And Isaac intreated the LORD for his wife, because she was barren: and the LORD was intreated of him, and Rebekah his wife conceived. And the children struggled together within her; and she said, If it be so, why am I thus? And she went to enquire of the LORD. And the LORD said unto her, Two nations are in thy womb, and two manner of people shall be separated from thy bowels; and the one people shall be stronger than the other people; and the elder shall serve the younger.*

Gen. 27:36-40 *And he said, Is not he rightly named Jacob? for he hath supplanted me these two times: he took away my birthright; and, behold, now he hath taken away my blessing. And he said, Hast thou not reserved a blessing for me? 37: And Isaac answered and said unto Esau, Behold, I have made him thy lord, and all his brethren have I given to him for servants; and with corn and wine have I sustained him: and what shall I do now unto thee, my son? And Esau said unto his father, Hast thou but one blessing, my father? bless me, even me also, O my father. And Esau lifted up his voice, and wept. And Isaac his father answered and said unto him, Behold, thy dwelling shall be the fatness of the earth, and of the dew of heaven from above; And by thy sword shalt thou live, and shalt serve thy brother; and it shall come to pass when thou shalt have the dominion, that thou shalt break his yoke from off thy neck.*

3.	Jacob's first child Reuben, did not receive the inheritance. It was given to JOSEPH.

 Gen. 49:3 *Reuben, thou art my firstborn, my might, and the beginning of my strength, the excellency of dignity, and the excellency of power.*

Gen. 48:21-22 *And Israel said unto Joseph, Behold, I die: but God shall be with you, and bring you again unto the land of your fathers.*

Gen 49:22-26. *Joseph is a fruitful bough, even a fruitful bough by a well; whose branches run over the wall: The archers have sorely grieved him, and shot at him, and hated him: But his bow abode in strength, and the arms of his hands were made strong by the hands of the mighty God of Jacob; (from thence is the shepherd, the stone of Israel:) Even by the God of thy father, who shall help thee; and by the Almighty, who shall bless thee with blessings of heaven above, blessings of the deep that lieth under, blessings of the breasts, and of the womb: The blessings of thy father have prevailed above the blessings of my progenitors unto the utmost bound of the everlasting hills: they shall be on the head of Joseph, and on the crown of the head of him that was separate from his brethren.*

4.	Joseph's first child, Manasseh, did not receive the inheritance. It was given to EPHRAIM.

Gen. 48:8-9 *And Israel beheld Joseph's sons, and said, Who are these? And Joseph said unto his father, They are my sons, whom God hath given me in this place. And he said, Bring them, I pray thee, unto me, and I will bless them.*

(Gen.17:19) *And when Joseph saw that his father laid his right hand upon the head of Ephraim, it displeased him: and he held up his father's hand, to remove it from Ephraim's head unto Manasseh's head. And Joseph said unto his father, Not so, my father: for this is the firstborn; put thy right hand upon his head. And his father refused, and said, I know it, my son, I know it: he also shall become a people, and he also shall be great: but truly his younger brother shall be greater than he, and his seed shall become a multitude of nations.*

5.	The first son of Jesse, Eliab, did not receive the inheritance.

It was given to DAVID,
(1 Samuel 16:6) *And it came to pass, when they were come, that he looked on Eliab, and said, Surely the LORD's anointed is before him.*
1Sam.11:13. *And Samuel said unto Jesse, Are here all thy children? And he said, There remaineth yet the youngest, and, behold, he keepeth the sheep. And Samuel said unto Jesse, Send and fetch him: for we will not sit down till he come hither. And he sent, and brought him in. Now he was ruddy, and withal of a beautiful countenance, and goodly to look to. And the LORD said, Arise, anoint him: for this is he. Then Samuel took the horn of oil, and anointed him in the midst of his brethren: and the Spirit of the LORD came upon David from that day forward. So Samuel rose up, and went to Ramah.*

6.   David's first son, Absalom, didn't receive the inheritance. It was given to SOLOMON.
(1 chronicle 22:6-12) *Then he called for Solomon his son, and charged him to build an house for the LORD God of Israel. And David said to Solomon, My son, as for me, it was in my mind to build an house unto the name of the LORD my God: But the word of the LORD came to me, saying, Thou hast shed blood abundantly, and hast made great wars: thou shalt not build an house unto my name, because thou hast shed much blood upon the earth in my sight. Behold, a son shall be born to thee, who shall be a man of rest; and I will give him rest from all his enemies round about: for his name shall be Solomon, and I will give peace and quietness unto Israel in his days. He shall build an house for my name; and he shall be my son, and I will be his father; and I will establish throne of his kingdom over Israel for ever. Now, my son, the LORD be with thee; and prosper thou, and build the house of the LORD thy God, as he hath said of thee. Only the LORD give thee wisdom and understanding, and give thee charge concerning Israel, that thou mayest keep the law of the LORD thy God.*
 (1 chronicle 23:1) *So when David was old and full of days, he made Solomon his son king over Israel*

7.   Judah (the son of Jacob's) first born could not make it with

the inheritance. It was given to PHAREZ from the womb.

(Gen. 38:26-30) *And Judah acknowledged them, and said, She hath been more righteous than I; because that I gave her not to Shelah my son. And he knew her again no more. And it came to pass in the time of her travail, that, behold, twins were in her womb. And it came to pass, when she travailed, that the one put out his hand: and the midwife took and bound upon his hand a scarlet thread, saying, This came out first, And it came to pass, as he drew back his hand, that, behold, his brother came out: and she said, How hast thou broken forth? This breach be upon thee: therefore his name was called Pharez. And afterward came out his brother, that had the scarlet thread upon his hand: and his name was called Zarah.*

Note: Judah was to produce a king for Israel in his generation by inheritance.

(Gen 49:10) *The sceptre shall not depart from Judah, nor a lawgiver from between his feet, until Shiloh come; and unto him shall the gathering of the people be. (The sceptre shall not depart from him). But because he committed extra marital affairs (incess) he could not produce the king for Israel for ten generations. — WHY? Because the scripture said that a Bastard shall not enter into the congregation of the lord to his tenth generation.*

(Deut. 23:2) *A bastard shall not enter into the congregation of the LORD; even to his tenth generation shall he not enter into the congregation of the LORD.*

(Matthew 1:1-6) *The book of the generation of Jesus Christ, the son of David, the son of Abraham. Abraham begat Isaac; and Isaac begat Jacob; and Jacob begat Judas and his brethren; And Judas begat Phares and Zara of Thamar; and Phares begat Esrom; and Esrom begat Aram; And Aram begat Aminadab; and Aminadab begat Naasson; and Naasson begat Salmon; And Salmon begat Booz of Rachab; and Booz begat Obed of Ruth; and Obed begat Jesse; And Jesse begat David the king; and David the king begat Solomon of her* *that had been the wife of Urias;*

C: Deadly rooted nature or attitude that destroys a given generation.

Case study 1: Abraham's family

Focus: Abraham and Abram went down into Egypt to sojourn there; for the famine was grievous in the land. And it came to pass, when he was come near to enter into Egypt, that he said unto Sarai his wife, Behold now, I know that thou art a fair woman to look upon: Therefore it shall come to pass, when the Egyptians shall see thee, that they shall say, This is his wife: and they will kill me, but they will save thee alive. Say, I pray thee, thou art my sister: that it may be well with me for thy sake; and my soul shall live because of thee. And it came to pass, that, when Abram was come into Egypt, the Egyptians beheld the woman that she was very fair.

- Spirit of lying **(Gen. 20:10-13)** *And Abimelech Abraham, What sawest thou, that thou hast done this thing? And Abraham said, Because I thought, Surely the fear of God is not in this place; and they will slay me for my wife's sake. And yet indeed she is my sister; she is the daughter of my father, but not the daughter of my mother; and she became my wife. And it came to pass, when God caused me to wander from my father's house, that I said unto her, This is thy kindness which thou shalt shew unto me; at every place whither we shall come, say of me, He is my brother.*
- Spirit of going after fair women
- Spirit of famine
- Spirit of Polygamy and marrying fair women
- Spirit of barrenness (25years)
- Spirit of repeated pattern of location/career

Case study 2: ISAAC

 And there was a famine in the land, beside the first famine that was in the days of Abraham. And Isaac went unto Abimelech king of the Philistines unto Gerar. And the LORD appeared unto him, and said, Go not down into Egypt; dwell in the land which I shall tell thee of: Sojourn in this land, and I will be with thee, and will bless thee; for unto thee, and unto thy seed, I will give all these countries, and I will perform the oath which I sware unto Abraham thy father; And I will make thy seed to multiply as the stars of heaven, and will give unto thy seed all these countries; and in thy seed shall all the nations of the earth be blessed;Because that Abraham obeyed my voice, and kept my charge, my commandments, my statutes, and my laws. And Isaac dwelt in Gerar: And the men of the place asked him of his wife; and he said, She is my sister: for he feared to say, She is my wife; lest, said he, the men of the place should kill me for Rebekah; because she was fair to look upon.

- Ø   Spirit of famine v 1:4
- Ø   Spirit of lying v 7
- Ø   Spirit of marrying fair women
- Ø   Spirit of fear vs7
- Ø   Spirit of barrenness **Gen. 25:21** *And Isaac intreated the LORD for his wife, because she was barren: and the LORD was intreated of him, and Rebekah his wife conceived.*

Case study 3: JACOB

Spirit of lying

Gen, 27:36 *And he said, is not he rightly named Jacob? for he hath supplanted me these two times: he took away my birthright; and, behold, now he hath taken away my blessing. And he said, Hast thou not reserved a blessing for me?*

v   Spirit of polygamy and marrying fair women

Gen.29:11, *And Jacob kissed Rachel, and lifted up his voice, and wept. Leah was tender eyed; but Rachel was beautiful and well favoured.*

Ge:29:18-20: *And Jacob loved Rachel; and said, I will serve thee seven years for Rachel thy younger daughter. And Laban said, It is better that I give her to thee, than that I should give her to another man: abide with me. And Jacob served seven years for Rachel; and they seemed unto him but a few days, for the love he had to her.*

v   Spirit of barrenness

Gen. 29:31 *And when the LORD saw that Leah was hated, he opened her womb: but Rachel was barren*

D: IDOLATORY IN THE FAMILY.

Psalm 16:4. *Their sorrows shall be multiplied that hasten after another god: their drink offerings of blood will I not offer, nor take up their names into my lips.*

Hosea.9:10-17. *I found Israel like grapes in the wilderness; I saw your fathers as the firstripe in the fig tree at her first time: but they went to Baal-peor, and separated themselves unto that shame; and their abominations were according as they loved. As for Ephraim, their glory shall fly away like a bird, from the birth, and from the womb, and from the conception. Though they bring up their children, yet will I bereave them, that there shall not be a man left: yea, woe also to them when I depart from them! Ephraim, as I saw Tyrus, is planted in a pleasant place: but Ephraim shall bring forth his children to the murderer. Give them, O LORD: what wilt thou give? give them a miscarrying womb and dry breasts. All their wickedness is in Gilgal: for there I hated them: for the wickedness of their doings I will drive them out of mine house, I will love them no more: all their princes are revolters. Ephraim is smitten, their root is dried up, they shall bear no fruit: yea, though they bring forth, yet will I slay even the beloved fruit of their womb. My God will cast them away, because they did not hearken unto him: and they shall be wanderers among the nations.*

- **THE EFFECTS OF IDOLATORY IN THE FAMILY.**
- **It causes barrenness and miscarriages.**

Hosea9:16-17 *Ephraim is smitten, their root is dried up, they shall bear no fruit: yea, though they bring forth, yet will I slay even the beloved fruit of their womb.17 My God will cast them away, because they did not hearken unto him: and they shall be wanderers among the nations.*

- **It leads to spiritual and physical enslavement.**

Psalm. 106:36-43. *And they served their idols: which were a snare unto them.37 Yea, they sacrificed their sons and their daughters unto devils, 38. And shed innocent blood, even the blood of their sons and of their daughters, whom they sacrificed unto the idols of Canaan: and the land was polluted with blood.*

39 Thus were they defiled with their own works, and went a whoring with their own inventions. 40. Therefore was the wrath of the LORD kindled against his people, in so much that he abhorred his own inheritance. 41. And he gave them into the hand of the heathen; and they that hated them ruled over them. 42. Their enemies also oppressed them, and they were brought into subjection under their hand. 43. Many times did he deliver them; but they provoked him with their counsel, and were brought low for their iniquity.

PRAYER POINT ON

A: THE INIQUITIES OF OUR FATHERS.

(Lamentation 5:7)

" *our fathers have sinned and are no more, but we borne their iniquities.*

- Lord, release the rain of the blood of Jesus into my family root and deliver me from all satanic inheritance.
- Tonight, by the fire of God I consume every satanic inheritance in my family.
- Every force that hinders people from raising their heads in my family, today I cut them down by the axe of God.
- I am ordained for greatness. I refuse to remain on the floor Tonight I enforce my enthronement by the blood of Jesus.

B: GENERATIONAL BATTLE OF THE FIRST BORN

Isaiah 26:11 *LORD, when thy hand is lifted up, they will not see: but they shall see, and be ashamed for their envy at the people; yea, the fire of thine enemies shall devour them*

Lord, tonight by your blood, I degree every family pattern destroying the destiny of men in my family be terminated.

*Today I curse the root of manipulation and enchantment in my family that moves people to do wrongs thing against their destiny.

* Lord, by the blood of Jesus, disconnect me and my family from every contrary force that has hindered my generation root.

* Lord, let the fire the enemy has set up against me and my children consume the enemy.
* By the blood of Jesus, I return the arrow of death afflictions, oppression, poverty and stagnation back to the camp of the enemy to destroy them without remedy in Jesus name.

C: DEADLY ROOTED NATURE OR ATTITUDE THAT DESTROYS A GIVEN GENERATION.

Spirit of fear And there was a famine in the land: and Abram went down into Egypt to sojourn there;.......

Spirit of lying **(Gen. 20:10-13)** *And Abimelech said unto Abraham, What sawest thou, that thou* **(Gen. 12:10-14)** *hast done this thing?*

- Lord, every generational power that controls the mind and character of a man to behave contrary to his destiny, today set me free.
- Lord, deliver me from generational weight that keeps a man on one spot.
- Lord, deliver me from powers that move my covenant helpers against me in the day of my favour.
- Lord, deliver me from every weakness that the devil uses to attack my generation and set me free today.

D: IDOLATORY IN THE FAMILY.

- Father, in the name of Jesus, deliver me permanently from the forces of idolatory that has held my family captive.
- Let the blood of Jesus, destroy every satanic covenant speaking over my life and destiny.

Chapter Two
Household Enemies

One of the greatest challenges of a man is the enemy of his household. So the bible declares.

Micah 7:6-8 *For the son dishonoureth the father, the daughter riseth up against her mother, the daughter in law against her mother in law; a man's enemies are the men of his own house. 7: Therefore I will look unto the LORD; I will wait for the God of my salvation: my God will hear me:8: Rejoice not against me, O mine enemy: when I fall, I shall arise; when I sit in darkness, the LORD shall be a light unto me.*

To be able to conquer household enemies, one must understand who they are and their mode of operation.

TYPES OF HOUSEHOLD ENEMIES

A. **Visible Household Enemies**: These are categories of household enemies that can be seen, identified by their location and deliberate act of wickedness, particularly among our family lineage. Sometimes, they pose to be friends and even express their concern towards you in moments of challenges or trials. They can go to the extent of being the force behind your troubles and still design a solution out of the trouble as a way of false pretence not to be suspected as the one behind your challenges.

How do they operate?

Visible household enemies operate constantly as a friend, to hide their original identity so as not to be suspected as the in-house enemy. They also get closer to their victims to obtain information about them, thereby using the same information as a trap to attack and afflict their victims.

(Proverb 27:6) *Faithful are the wounds of a friend; but the kisses of an enemy are deceitful.*

B.   **Invisible Household Enemies:**   these are categories of enemies around us which cannot be seen or identified, except God opens your spiritual eyes to see them. They constitute eighty percent of our spiritual battles, because they can be around us at home, work place, school, ministerial assignment, business transaction arena and the likes.

How do you handle them?

1. **By the mystery of prophetic declaration.**
    Ezekiel 11:13 *And it came to pass, when I prophesied, that Pelatiah the son of Benaiah died. Then fell I down upon my face, and cried with a loud voice, and said, Ah Lord GOD! wilt thou make a full end of the remnant of Israel?*
    Psalm 120:7 *I am for peace: but when I speak, they are for war.*
    Luke 21:15 *For I will give you a mouth and wisdom, which all your adversaries shall not be able to gainsay nor resist.*

2. **By the mystery of the blood of Jesus.**
    Hebrews 11:28 *Through faith he kept the passover, and the sprinkling of blood, lest he that destroyed the firstborn should touch them.*

3. **By the mystery of supernatural disconnection.**
    Micah 5:9 *Thine hand shall be lifted up upon thine adversaries, and all thine enemies shall be cut off.*

PRAYER POINT ON:
HANDLING HOUSEHOLD ENEMIES

1. Today, I send the fire of destruction into the foundation of my family. Anywhere the enemies of my household are hiding, lord roast them to death.
2. Today, I send the hammer of God against the gang up of evil men in my family Father, nail them to death.
3. Today, I release the warring angels of heaven into my family, root out every habitation of evil men, and consume them in their wickedness.
4. Today, I command the wild wind from the presence of God to blow all my household enemies into the sea of destruction forever.
5. Today, I receive the rivers of living water from the throne of God to wash me clean from every Satanic mark that has kept my life on a spot.
6. Today, I speak to the power of God that holds the universe to reverse every enchantment and manipulation that has been programmed into the air to control my life.
7. I decree the blood of Jesus, to purge my spirit, soul and body of every satanic deposit that has made my life uncomfortable.

CHAPTER THREE
FALSE PROPHETS

One of the principal agents used by devils to keep the lives of people under bondage is the agency of false prophets.

WHO ARE FALSE PROPHETS?

1. They are extension of witchcraft agents in religious garments.

(Rev. 16:13-14) *And I saw three unclean spirit like frogs come out of the mouth of the dragon, and out of the mouth of the beast and out of the mouth of the false prophet. For they are the spirit of devils, working miracles, which go forth unto the kings of the earth and of the whole world, to gather them to the battle of that great day of God Almighty.*

2. They are spiritual agents that lie to people using the name of God.

(Jer.23:21-29) *I have not sent these prophets, yet they ran: I have not spoken to them, yet they prophesied.: But if they had stood in my counsel, and had caused my people to hear my words, then they should have turned them from their evil way, and from the evil of their doings. Am I a God at hand, saith the LORD, and not a God afar off? Can any hide himself in secret places that I shall not see him? saith the LORD. Do not I fill heaven and earth? saith the LORD. I have heard what the prophets said, that prophesy lies in my name, saying, I have dreamed, I have dreamed.: How long shall this be in the heart of the prophets that prophesy lies? yea, they are prophets of the deceit of their own heart; Which think to cause my people to forget my name by their dreams which they tell every man to his neighbour, as their fathers have forgotten my name for Baal. The prophet that hath a dream, let him tell a dream; and he that hath my word, let him speak my word faithfully. What is the chaff to the wheat? saith the LORD. Is not my word like as a fire? saith the LORD; and like a hammer that breaketh the rock in pieces?*

3. **They are spiritual agents that enslave people with false dreams and visions under the cover of the spirit of God.**

Jer. 23-32 *Behold, I am against them that prophesy false dreams, saith the LORD, and do tell them, and cause my people to err by their lies, and by their lightness;*

Jer.23:26 *how long shall this be in the heart of the prophets that prophesy lies? yea, they are prophets of the deceit of their own heart.*

4. **They are self-employed and self-arranged title prophets.**

Jer. 23-32b *yet I sent them not, nor commanded them: therefore they shall not profit this people at all, saith the LORD.*

CHARACTERISTICS OF FALSE PROPHETS

1.   **They prophesy lies.** *(Jer. 14:13-15) Then said I, Ah, Lord GOD! behold, the prophets say unto them, Ye shall not see the sword, neither shall ye have famine; but I will give you assured peace in this place. Then the LORD said unto me, The prophets prophesy lies in my name: I sent them not, neither have I commanded them, neither spake unto them: they prophesy unto you a false vision and divination, and a thing of nought, and the deceit of their heart. Therefore thus saith the LORD concerning the prophets that prophesy in my name, and I sent them not, yet they say, Sword and famine shall not be in this land; By sword and famine shall those prophets be consumed.*

2.   **They see false vision.** *(Ezekie13:1-10) And the word of the LORD came unto me, saying, Son of man, prophesy against the prophets of Israel that prophesy, and say thou unto them that prophesy out of their own hearts, Hear ye the word of the LORD; Thus saith the Lord GOD; Woe unto the foolish prophets, that follow their own spirit, and have seen nothing! O Israel, thy prophets are like the foxes in the deserts. Ye have not gone up into the gaps, neither made up the hedge for the house of Israel to stand in the battle in the day of the LORD. They have seen vanity and lying divination, saying, The LORD saith: and the LORD hath not sent them: and they have made others to hope that they would confirm the word. Have ye not seen a vain vision, and have ye not spoken a lying divination, whereas ye say, The LORD saith it; albeit I have not spoken? Therefore thus saith the Lord GOD; Because ye have spoken vanity, and seen lies, therefore, behold, I am against you, saith the Lord GOD. And mine hand shall be upon the prophets that see vanity, and that divine lies: they shall not be in the assembly of my people, neither shall they be written in the*

writing of the house of Israel, neither shall they enter into the land of Israel; and ye shall know that I am the Lord GOD. Because, even because they have seduced my people, saying, Peace; and there was no peace; and one built up a wall, and, lo, others daubed it with untempered morter:

3.   **They use false powers from the mouth of the false prophet. (Rev. 16:13-14)** *And I saw three unclean spirit like frogs come out of the mouth of the dragon, and out of the mouth of the beast and out of the mouth of the false prophet. For they are the spirit of devils, working miracles, which go forth unto the kings of the earth and of the whole world, to gather them to the battle of that great day of God Almighty.*

4.   **They perform false miracles (2 thes. 2:8-10)** *And then shall that Wicked be revealed, whom the Lord shall consume with the spirit of his mouth, and shall destroy with the brightness of his coming: Even him, whose coming is after the working of Satan with all power and signs and lying wonders, And with all deceivableness of unrighteousness in them that perish; because they received not the love of the truth, that they might be saved.*

5.   **They lead people into errors. (Is 9:14-17)** *Therefore the LORD will cut off from Israel head and tail, branch and rush, in one day. The ancient and honourable, he is the head; and the prophet that teacheth lies, he is the tail. For the leaders of this people cause them to err; and they that are led of them are destroyed. Therefore the Lord shall have no joy in their young men, neither shall have mercy on their fatherless and widows: for everyone is an hypocrite and an evildoer, and every mouth speaketh folly. For all this his anger is not turned away, but his hand is stretched out still.*

WHAT ARE THE WEAKNESSES OF THESE FALSE PROPHETS?

1. **What they prophesy**: The vision they see, the power they operate with and the miracles they perform do not stand the test of time.
2. **Lack of permanent solutions**: Most of the times they see problems, but they hardly produce a permanent answer to the foreseen troubles.
3. **Multiplied challenges**: Often times, the problems are multiplied.
4. **They don't end well.**

How does God handles the operations of false prophets?

1. The Lord shall cut them off, He will consume them with the spirit of his mouth. **(2 Thes.2:8)** *And then shall that Wicked be revealed, whom the Lord shall consume with the spirit of his mouth, and shall destroy with the brightness of his coming:*

Prayer points

1. Anywhere they have taken my name, picture, career, destiny to, for spiritual ritual, Oh God of vengeance consume them in your anger today.
2. Anything the false prophet has said over my head, destiny, marriage, business, let the fire of God consume it today.
3. Lord today cut off every covenant that has been made on my behalf through a false prophet.
4. Lord today, destroy every power that moves against a man to be unfortunate in the day of his miracle and destroy the force of manipulation that keeps a man late in day of his appointment.

5. By a forceful hand from the throne of God, usher me speedily to my next level of glory and honour.

Chapter Four
The Power of Vision

WHAT IS VISION?

In the context of dreams and trance, it can be defined as:

·   The voice of God communicating to man through pictures and symbols.

·   Having an encounter with the supernatural beings presenting to you a message from God.

Hosea 12:10 I have also spoken by the prophets, and I have multiplied visions, and used similitudes, by the ministry of the prophets.

TYPES OF VISIONS.

1.   **Dreams:** These are revelations shown to you by God when you are sleeping.

Types of dreams:

Ø   **Specific Dreams:** This is the kind of revelation shown to you when you are sleeping. And the revelation came to pass exactly the way you saw it. **(Matthew. 1:18-25)** *But forasmuch as he had not to pay, his lord commanded him to be sold, and his wife, and children, and all that he had, and payment to be made.* (emphasis on verse 20, 24).

It is also a confirmation of the move of God about something or a place that you can't see with your physical eyes but, made known unto you in the dream.

Ø   **Symbolic Dreams:** When God show you something in the dream using a different object, but retaining its meaning and purpose in the physical.

Judges 7:9-16 *And it came to pass the same night, that the LORD said unto him, Arise, get thee down unto the host; for I have delivered it into thine hand. But if thou fear to go down, go thou with Phurah thy servant down to the host: And thou shalt hear what they say; and afterward shall thine hands be strengthened to go down unto the host. Then went he down with Phurah his servant unto the outside of the armed men that were in the host. And the Midianites and the Amalekites and all the children of the east lay along in the valley like grasshoppers for multitude; and their camels were without number, as the sand by the sea side for multitude. And when Gideon was come, behold, there was a man that told a dream unto his fellow, and said, Behold, I dreamed a dream, and, lo, a cake of barley bread tumbled into the host of Midian, and came unto a tent, and smote it that it fell, and overturned it, that the tent lay along. And his fellow answered and said, This is nothing else save the sword of Gideon the son of Joash, a man of Israel: for into his hand hath God delivered Midian, and all the host. And it was so, when Gideon heard the telling of the dream, and the interpretation thereof, that he worshipped, and returned into the host of Israel, and said, Arise; for the LORD hath delivered into your hand the host of Midian. And he divided the three hundred men into three companies, and he put a trumpet in every man's hand, with empty pitchers, and lamps within the pitchers*
.

   Ø **Contradictory Dreams**: when your dream speaks exact opposite of what you saw happening in the physical.

(Gen.41:1-8) *And it came to pass at the end of two full years, that Pharaoh dreamed: and, behold, he stood by the river. And, behold, there came up out of the river seven well favoured kine and fatfleshed; and they fed in a meadow. And, behold, seven other kine came up after them out of the river, ill-favoured and leanfleshed; and stood by the other kine upon the brink of the river. And the ill-favoured and leanfleshed kine did eat up the seven well favoured and fat kine. So Pharaoh awoke. And he slept and dreamed the second time: and, behold, seven* *ears of corn came up upon one stalk, rank and good. And, behold, seven thin ears and blasted with the east wind sprung up after them. And the seven thin ears devoured the seven rank and full ears. And Pharaoh awoke, and, behold, it was a dream. And it came to pass in the morning that his spirit was troubled; and he sent and called for all the magicians of Egypt, and all the wise men thereof: and Pharaoh told them his dream; but there was none that could interpret them unto Pharaoh. dream of pharaoh, 7 sick cattle and 7 wealthy, 7 sickly cow and 7 healthy cow. Burning house-commission house, crying in the dream- wedding, failure in exam-success,*

Ø **Manipulative Dreams:** This is a situation where the agents of darkness (herbalists, witches, and false prophets) use your dreams to destroy your destiny. e.g.

a. Dead people could appear and be talking to you.
b. Someone collecting money from you anytime you are about to collect salary.
c. Someone cuts your body with an object.
d. Bitten by a snake in the dream.
e. Eating in the dream.

Ø **Corrupted Dreams:** Inability to remember the dreams you had and sometimes such dreams have no specific direction and interpretation. In such situation, it takes the finger of God to bring a meaning out of that kind of dream.

(Dan.2:1-5) *And in the second year of the reign of Nebuchadnezzar Nebuchadnezzar dreamed dreams, wherewith his spirit was troubled, and his sleep brake from him. Then the king commanded to call the magicians, and the astrologers, and the sorcerers, and the Chaldeans, for to shew the king his dreams. So they came and stood before the king. And the king said unto them, I have dreamed a dream, and my spirit was troubled to know the dream. Then spake the Chaldeans to the king in Syriack, O king, live for ever: tell thy servants the* *dream, and we will shew the interpretation. The king answered and said to the Chaldeans, The thing is gone from me: if ye will not make known unto me the dream, with the interpretation thereof, ye shall be cut in pieces, and your houses shall be made a dunghill.*

WHAT IS A TRANCE

It is the kind of vision you see with your eyes opened. For that moment you are suspended from the physical environment.

Act 10:1-3 There was a certain man in Caesarea called Cornelius, a centurion of the band called the Italian band, A devout man, and one that feared God with all his house, which gave much alms to the people, and prayed to God alway. He saw in a vision evidently about the ninth hour of the day an angel of God coming in to him, and saying unto him, Cornelius.

Acts 10:10-11 *And he became very hungry, and would have eaten: but while they made ready, he fell into a trance, And saw heaven opened, and a certain vessel descending unto him, as it had been a great sheet knit at the four corners, and let down to the earth.*

Type of trance

A. Specific trance: The way God communicated with you (or appear to you) exactly the same way it came to pass.

(Judges 13:1-13) *And the children of Israel did evil again in the sight of the LORD; and the LORD delivered them into the hand of the Philistines forty years. And there was a certain man of Zorah, of the family of the Danites, whose name was Manoah; and his wife was barren, and bare not. And the angel of the LORD appeared unto the woman, and said unto her, Behold now, thou art barren, and bearest not: but thou shalt conceive, and bear a son. Now therefore beware, I pray thee, and drink not wine nor strong drink, and eat not any unclean thing: For, lo, thou shalt conceive, and bear a son; and no razor shall come on his head: for the child shall be a Nazarite* *unto God from the womb: and he shall begin to deliver Israel out of the hand of the Philistines. Then the woman came and told her husband, saying, A man of God came unto me, and his countenance was like the countenance of an angel of God, very terrible: but I asked him not whence he was, neither told he me his name: But he said unto me, Behold, thou shalt conceive, and bear a son; and now drink no wine nor strong drink, neither eat any unclean thing: for the child shall be a Nazarite to God from the womb to the day of his death. Then Manoah intreated the LORD, and said, O my Lord, let the man of God which thou didst send come again unto us, and teach us what we shall do unto the child that shall be born. And God hearkened to the voice of Manoah; and the angel of God came again unto the woman as she sat in the field: but Manoah her husband was not with her. And the woman made haste, and ran, and shewed her husband, and said unto him, Behold, the man hath appeared unto me, that came unto me the other day. And Manoah arose, and went after his wife, and came to the man, and said unto him, Art thou the man that spakest unto the woman? And he said, I am. And Manoah said, Now let thy words come to pass. How shall we order the child, and how shall we do unto him? And the angel of the LORD said unto Manoah, Of all that I said unto the woman let her beware.*

(Act 10:1-8.) *There was a certain man in Caesarea called Cornelius, a centurion of the band called the Italian band, A devout man, and one that feared God with all his house, which gave much alms to the people, and prayed to God alway. He saw in a vision evidently about the ninth hour of the day an angel of God coming in to him, and saying unto him, Cornelius. And when he looked on him, he was afraid, and said, What is it, Lord? And he said unto him, Thy prayers and thine alms are come up for a memorial before God. And now send men to Joppa, and call for one Simon, whose surname is Peter: He lodgeth with one Simon a tanner, whose house is by the sea side: he shall tell thee what thou oughtest to do. And when the angel which spake unto Cornelius was departed, he called two of his household servants, and a devout soldier of them that waited on him continually; And when he had declared all these things unto them, he sent them to Joppa.*

B.	Symbolic Trance: *it is God giving you the picture of what is to happen, but require accurate interpretation.*

(Act.10:9-33.) *On the morrow, as they went on their journey, and drew nigh unto the city, Peter went up upon the housetop to pray about the sixth hour: And he became very hungry, and would have eaten: but while they made ready, he fell into a trance, And saw heaven opened, and a certain vessel descending unto him, as it had been a great sheet knit at the four corners, and let down to the earth: Wherein were all manner of fourfooted beasts of the earth, and wild beasts, and creeping things, and fowls of the air. And there came a voice to him, Rise, Peter; kill, and eat. But Peter said, Not so, Lord; for I have never eaten anything that is common or unclean. And the voice spake unto him again the second time, What God hath cleansed, that call not thou common. This was done thrice: and the vessel was received up again into heaven. Now while Peter doubted in himself what this vision which he had seen should mean, behold, the men which were sent from Cornelius had made enquiry for Simon's house, and stood before the gate, And called, and asked whether Simon, which was surnamed Peter, were lodged there. While Peter thought on the vision, the Spirit said unto him, Behold, three men seek thee. Arise therefore, and get thee down, and go with them, doubting nothing: for I have sent them. Then Peter went down to the men which were sent unto him from Cornelius; and said, Behold, I am he whom ye seek: what is the cause wherefore ye are come? And they said, Cornelius the centurion, a just man, and one that feareth God, and of good report among all the nation of the Jews, was warned from God by an holy angel to send for thee into his house, and to hear words of thee. Then called he them in, and lodged them. And on the morrow Peter went away with them, and certain brethren from Joppa accompanied him. And the morrow after they entered into Caesarea. And Cornelius waited for them, and had called together his kinsmen and near friends. And as Peter was coming in, Cornelius met him, and fell down at his feet, and worshipped him. But Peter took him up, saying, Stand up; I myself also am a man. And as he talked with him, he went in, and found many that* *were come together. And he said unto them, Ye know how that it is an unlawful thing for a man that is a Jew to keep company, or come unto one of another nation; but God hath shewed me that I should not call any man common or unclean. Therefore came I unto you without gainsaying, as soon as I was sent for: I ask therefore for what intent ye have sent for me? And Cornelius said, Four days ago I was fasting until this hour; and at the ninth hour I prayed in my house, and, behold, a man stood before me in bright clothing, And said, Cornelius, thy prayer is heard, and thine alms are had in remembrance in the sight of God. Send therefore to Joppa, and call hither Simon, whose surname is Peter; he is lodged in the house of one Simon a tanner by the sea side: who, when he cometh, shall speak unto thee. Immediately therefore I sent to thee; and thou hast well done that thou art come. Now therefore are we all here present before God, to hear all things that are commanded thee of God.*

(Dan. 5: 1-6) *Belshazzar the king made a great feast to a thousand of his lords, and drank wine before the thousand. Belshazzar, whiles he tasted the wine, commanded to bring the golden and silver vessels which his father Nebuchadnezzar had taken out of the temple which was in Jerusalem; that the king, and his princes, his wives, and his concubines, might drink therein. Then they brought the golden vessels that were taken out of the temple of the house of God which was at Jerusalem; and the king, and his princes, his wives, and his concubines, drank in them. They drank wine, and praised the gods of gold, and of silver, of brass, of iron, of wood, and of stone. In the same hour came forth fingers of a man's hand, and wrote over against the candlestick upon the plaister of the wall of the king's palace: and the king saw the part of the hand that wrote. Then the king's countenance was changed, and his thoughts troubled him, so that the joints of his loins were loosed, and his knees smote one against another. (v22-25) And thou his son, O Belshazzar, hast not humbled thine heart, though thou knewest all this;Da:5:23: But hast lifted up thyself against the LORD of heaven; and they have brought the vessels of his house before thee, and thou, and thy lords, thy wives, and thy concubines, have drunk wine in them; and thou hast* *praised the gods of silver, and gold, of brass, iron, wood, and stone, which see not, nor hear, nor know: and the God in whose hand thy breath is, and whose are all thy ways, hast thou not glorified: Then was the part of the hand sent from him; and this writing was written. And this is the writing that was written, MENE, MENE, TEKEL, UPHARSIN.*

C.   **Manipulative Trance:** *ability to see strange forces that others cannot see manifesting through the spirit of devils.*
Act.19:13-16 Then certain of the vagabond Jews, exorcists, took upon them to call over them which had evil spirits the name of the Lord Jesus, saying, We adjure you by Jesus whom Paul preacheth. And there were seven sons of one Sceva, a Jew, and chief of the priests, which did so. And the evil spirit answered and said, Jesus I know, and Paul I know; but who are ye? And the man in whom the evil spirit was leaped on them, and overcame them, and prevailed against them, so that they fled out of that house naked and wounded.

D.   Manipulative voice: *Ability to hear strange voices that others could not hear manifesting through the spirit of devils.*
(Act.16:16-19) *And it came to pass, as we went to prayer, a certain damsel possessed with a spirit of divination met us, which brought her masters much gain by soothsaying: The same followed Paul and us, and cried, saying, These men are the servants of the most high God, which shew unto us the way of salvation. And this did she many days. But Paul, being grieved, turned and said to the spirit, I command thee in the name of Jesus Christ to come out of her. And he came out the same hour. And when her masters saw that the hope of their gains was gone, they caught Paul and Silas, and drew them into the marketplace unto the rulers,*

PRAYER POINTS ON:
VISIONS: DREAMS AND TRANCE.

Ø   Lord, by the blood of Jesus, open my spiritual eyes to see what my physical eyes can't see that the devil uses against my destiny.

Ø Lord, everything the enemy has planted into my system in the dream to destroy my body, by the blood of Jesus flush it out.

Ø Lord everything that has been deposited into my destiny, not to move forward in life, Jesus root it out today.

Ø Lord, everything I have eaten and collected in the dream that has scattered my destiny, Jesus reverse it today.

Ø Lord, I set on fire every form of manipulation, enchantment and divination that held down the destiny of my family members.

Ø Lord, this week appear to my enemies in a terrible way and fight my battles for me.

Ø Lord, from today appear to me in a way that I will hear and understand you.

Ø By the blood of Jesus, heal me of spiritual blindness. Connect me to the place of divine revelation that will move my life forward.

Ø Lord I want an encounter from heaven that will turnaround my life permanently.

Ø By the blood of Jesus, open my eyes to understand the solution to my life challenges.

Ø Lord, double my spiritual power to conquer every opposition in the realm of the spirit.

Ø Lord, let my family spiritual altar catch a fresh fire to the glory of God.

Chapter Five
Engaging the Power of an Angel

According to the law of creation, Man is made lower than Angels. Yet, by covenant, man through the work of redemption is empowered to give command to Angels to carry out specific spiritual assignment.

Psalm 8:4-5 *What is man, that thou art mindful of him? and the son of man, that thou visitest him? For thou hast made him a little lower than the angels, and hast crowned him with glory and honour.*
Hebrews 1:7, 14 And of the angels he saith, Who maketh his angels spirits, and his ministers a flame of fire. (14) Are they not all ministering spirits, sent forth to minister for them who shall be heirs of salvation?

Who are angels?
1. They are supernatural beings with celestial or immortal bodies. They can enter anywhere anytime, appear and disappear.
Ps. 104:4, *Who maketh his angels spirits; his ministers a flaming fire:*
Heb. 1:7. *And of the angels he saith, Who maketh his angels spirits, and his ministers a flame of fire.*

2. They are carriers of God's message to mankind.

Case Study A: Joseph
Matt. 1: 20 *But while he thought on these things, behold, the angel of the Lord appeared unto him in a dream, saying, Joseph, thou son of David, fear not to take unto thee Mary thy wife: for that which is conceived in her is of the Holy Ghost.*

Case Study B: Zechariah
Luke. 1:9-13 *According to the custom of the priest's office, his lot was to burn*

incense when he went into the temple of the Lord. And the whole multitude of the people were praying without at the time of incense. And there appeared unto him an angel of the Lord standing on the right side of the altar of incense. And when Zacharias saw him, he was troubled, and fear fell upon him. But the angel said unto him, Fear not, Zacharias: for thy prayer is heard; and thy wife Elisabeth shall bear thee a son, and thou shalt call his name John.

Case Study C: Mary
Luke 1:26-30 *And in the sixth month the angel Gabriel was sent from God unto a city of Galilee, named Nazareth, To a virgin espoused to a man whose name was Joseph, of the house of David; and the virgin's name was Mary. And the angel came in unto her, and said, Hail, thou that art highly favoured, the Lord is with thee: blessed art thou among women. And when she saw him, she was troubled at his saying, and cast in her mind what manner of salutation this should be. And the angel said unto her, Fear not, Mary: for thou hast found favour with God.*

3. They are divine visitors on earth that come in form of a man. **Heb. 13:1-2** *Let brotherly love continue. Be not forgetful to entertain strangers: for thereby some have entertained angels unawares. (Archbishop Idahosa)*

4. They are helpers of men.
Luke 22.42-43) *Saying, Father, if thou be willing, remove this cup from me: nevertheless not my will, but thine, be done. Lu:22:43: And there appeared an angel unto him from heaven, strengthening him.*

5. They are co-worshippers in Zion .
Hebrews 12:22. *But ye are come unto mount Sion, and unto the city of the living God, the heavenly Jerusalem, and to an innumerable company of angels,*

6. They are agents of rescue and destruction. **Act. 12:1-11,** *Now about*

that time Herod the king stretched forth his hands to vex certain of the church.
Ac:12:2: *And he killed James the brother of John with the sword. And because he saw it pleased the Jews, he proceeded further to take Peter also. (Then were the days of unleavened bread.) And when he had apprehended him, he put him in prison, and delivered him to four quaternions of soldiers to keep him; intending after Easter to bring him forth to the people. Peter therefore was kept in prison: but prayer was made without ceasing of the church unto God for him. And when Herod would have brought him forth, the same night Peter was sleeping between two soldiers, bound with two chains: and the keepers before the door kept the prison. And, behold, the angel of the Lord came upon him, and a light shined in the prison: and he smote Peter on the side, and raised him up, saying, Arise up quickly. And his chains fell off from his hands. And the angel said unto him, Gird thyself, and bind on thy sandals. And so he did. And he saith unto him, Cast thy garment about thee, and follow me. And he went out, and followed him; and wist not that it was true which was done by the angel; but thought he saw a vision. When they were past the first and the second ward, they came unto the iron gate that leadeth unto the city; which opened to them of his own accord: and they went out, and passed on through one street; and forthwith the angel departed from him. And when Peter was come to himself, he said, now I know of a surety, that the Lord hath sent his angel, and hath delivered me out of the hand of Herod, and from all the expectation of the people of the Jews. Peter and angel of rescue)*
Psalm 34:4-7 *I sought the LORD, and he heard me, and delivered me from all my fears. They looked unto him, and were lightened: and their faces were not ashamed. This poor man cried, and the LORD heard him, and saved him out of all his troubles. The angel of the LORD encampeth round about them that fear him, and delivereth them.*

Psalm.35:3-6 *Draw out also the spear, and stop the way against them that persecute me: say unto my soul, I am thy salvation. Let them be confounded and put to shame that seek after my soul: let them be turned back and brought to confusion that devise my hurt. Let them be as chaff before the wind: and let the* *angel of the LORD chase them.: Let their way be dark and slippery: and let the angel of the LORD persecute them.*

7. They are spiritual messengers for the saint.
Heb. 1:14 Are they not all ministering spirits, sent forth to minister for them who shall be heirs of salvation?

HOW DO I ENGAGE ANGELS FOR DIVINE INTERVENTION
Principally Among other things
A. **By the word Psalm 103:20** *Bless the LORD, ye his angels that excel in strength, that do his commandments, hearkening unto the voice of his word.*

B. **By the blood Ex. 12: 23** *For the LORD will pass through to smite the Egyptians; and when he seeth the blood upon the lintel, and on the two side posts, the LORD will pass over the door, and will not suffer the destroyer to come in unto your houses to smite you.*

C. **By giving them command. Heb.1:14** *Are they not all ministering spirits, sent forth to minister for them who shall be heirs of salvation?*

The Limitation of an Angel
They are spiritual messengers that must not be worshipped.
(Rev.19:10). *And I fell at his feet to worship him. And he said unto me, See thou do it not: I am thy fellowservant, and of thy brethren that have the testimony of Jesus: worship God: for the testimony of Jesus is the spirit of prophecy.*

What Is the Capacity of an Angel?
1. **Angels have great powers. Rev.18:1-2.** *And after these things I saw another angel come down from heaven, having great power; and the earth was lightened with his glory. And he cried mightily with a strong voice, saying, Babylon the great is fallen, is fallen, and is become the habitation of devils, and the hold of every foul spirit, and a cage of every unclean and hateful bird.*

2. **Angels give divine direction. Ex. 23:20**. *Behold, I send an Angel before thee, to keep thee in the way, and to bring thee into the place which I have prepared.*

3. **Angels can stop your enemies from attacking you. (Num. 22.21-28)** *And Balaam rose up in the morning, and saddled his ass, and went with the princes of Moab.: And God's anger was kindled because he went: and the angel of the LORD stood in the way for an adversary against him. Now he was riding upon his ass, and his two servants were with him. And the ass saw the angel of the LORD standing in the way, and his sword drawn in his hand: and the ass turned aside out of the way, and went into the field: and Balaam smote the ass, to turn her into the way. But the angel of the LORD stood in a path of the vineyards, a wall being on this side, and a wall on that side. And when the ass saw the angel of the LORD, she thrust herself unto the wall, and crushed Balaam's foot against the wall: and he smote her again. And the angel of the LORD went further, and stood in a narrow place, where was no way to turn either to the right hand or to the left.: And when the ass saw the angel of the LORD, she fell down under Balaam: and Balaam's anger was kindled, and he smote the ass with a staff. And the LORD opened the mouth of the ass, and she said unto Balaam, What have I done unto thee, that thou hast smitten me these three times?*

4. **Angels are divine helpers Gen. 32:11-12** *Deliver me, I pray thee, from the hand of my brother, from the hand of Esau: for I fear him, lest he will come and smite me, and the mother with the children. And thou saidst, I will surely do thee good, and make thy seed as the sand of the sea, which cannot be numbered for multitude.*

5. **Angels contends with your enemies to deliver your miracle. Dan. 10:11-13.** *And, behold, an hand touched me, which set me upon my knees and upon the palms of my hands.Da:10:11: And he said unto me, O Daniel, a man greatly beloved, understand the words that I speak unto thee, and stand upright: for unto thee am I now sent.*

And when he had spoken this word unto me, I stood trembling. Then said he unto me, Fear not, Daniel: for from the first day that thou didst set thine heart to understand, and to chasten thyself before thy God, thy words were heard, and I am come for thy words. But the prince of the kingdom of Persia withstood me one and twenty days: but, lo, Michael, one of the chief princes, came to help me; and I remained there with the kings of Persia.

6. **Angels have power to impact you with talent, gifts and understanding. (Daniel 9:21-22)** *Yea, whiles I was speaking in prayer, even the man Gabriel, whom I had seen in the vision at the beginning, being caused to fly swiftly, touched me about the time of the evening oblation.Da:9:22: And he informed me, and talked with me, and said, O Daniel, I am now come forth to give thee skill and understanding.*

7. **Angels can cut off all the mighty enemies of your life. (2 Chronicle 32:20-24)** *And for this cause Hezekiah the king, and the prophet Isaiah the son of Amoz, prayed and cried to heaven. And the LORD sent an angel, which cut off all the mighty men of valour, and the leaders and captains in the camp of the king of Assyria. So he returned with shame of face to his own land. And when he was come into the house of his god, they that came forth of his own bowels slew him there with the sword. Thus the LORD saved Hezekiah and the inhabitants of Jerusalem from the hand of Sennacherib the king of Assyria, and from the hand of all other, and guided them on every side.: And many brought gifts unto the LORD to Jerusalem, and presents to Hezekiah king of Judah: so that he was magnified in the sight of all nations from thenceforth. In those days Hezekiah was sick to the death, and prayed unto the LORD: and he spake unto him, and he gave him a sign.*

8. Angels can engage in battle for an hour, a day, a month, and a year.
Rev. 9:15 *And the four angels were loosed, which were prepared for an hour, and a day, and a month, and a year, for to slay the third part of men.*

9. Angels can strengthen you in the place of prayer. Luke 22:43
And there appeared an angel unto him from heaven, strengthening him.

PRAYER POINT ON:
ENGAGING THE POWER OF AN ANGEL
1.   Lord, bring me out of the prison of life through the hand of an angel. Let the blood speak victory and deliverance over my destiny.
2.   Lord, by the covenant of the blood of Jesus, I decree that God should persecute every enemy of my destiny.
3.   Lord, beginning from this day anywhere I sprinkle this blood, let the angels of God take over my matter.
4.   Lord, by the hand of an angel deliver my good news and that of my family speedily this month in Jesus name.
5.   Lord, through the ministry of an angel give me a life time encounter that will change the story of my life forever.
6.   Lord, by the power of your blood, I send the angels on assignment to arrest all household enemies physical, spiritual and bring them under divine judgement.
7.   Lord, today I engage the great power of God through the ministry of angels to bring down the camp of my enemies by fire and thunder.
8.   By the power of the blood of Jesus, I decree the waiting angels of God to stand between me and all invisible enemies and bring them total destruction.
9.   By the blood of Jesus, I receive direction for my family,

career and destiny through the help of an angel.

10. By the hand of an angel I receive my long awaited miracle and blessings.

11. Today, Lord please send your angel to touch my body, soul and spirit and heal me from all afflictions and infirmities.

CHAPTER SIX
THE POWER OF A SPOKEN WORD

- What gives the supernatural motion for strange manifestation is the might of a spoken word. Power in the realm of the spirit remains dormant without a spoken word.
- The spoken word has the capacity to determine what happens to a man, either good or bad.
- The power of a spoken word is not in the power itself, but the might of the word in power.
- Therefore, if God wants to manifest through you, your mouth (which is your weapon) must equate with your word.

Types of negative words that can cage a man.

Case study: 1

Personal pronouncement against the enemy. Luke 21:12-15 *But before all these, they shall lay their hands on you, and persecute you, delivering you up to the synagogues, and into prisons, being brought before kings and rulers for my name's sake. And it shall turn to you for a testimony. Settle it therefore in your hearts, not to meditate before what ye shall answer: For I will give you a mouth and wisdom, which all your adversaries shall not be able to gainsay nor resist.*

(Ecc.8:4. Where the word of a king is, there is power: and who may say unto him, What doest thou?

Case study: 2

Personal pronouncement against yourself.

Num.30:1-16 And Moses spake unto the heads of the tribes concerning the children of Israel, saying, This is the thing which the LORD hath commanded. If a man vow a vow unto the LORD, or swear an oath to bind his soul with a bond; he shall not break his word, he shall do according to all that proceedeth out of his mouth.

.Nu:30:3: If a woman also vow a vow unto the LORD, and bind herself by a bond, being in her father's house in her youth; And her father hear her vow, and her bond wherewith she hath bound her soul, and her father shall hold his peace at her: then all her vows shall stand, and every bond wherewith she hath bound her soul shall stand. But if her father disallow her in the day that he heareth; not any of her vows, or of her bonds wherewith she hath bound her soul, shall stand: and the LORD shall forgive her, because her father disallowed her. And if she had at all an husband, when she vowed, or uttered ought out of her lips, wherewith she bound her soul; And her husband heard it, and held his peace at her in the day that he heard it: then her vows shall stand, and her bonds wherewith she bound her soul shall stand. But if her husband disallowed her on the day that he heard it; then he shall make her vow which she vowed, and that which she uttered with her lips, wherewith she bound her soul, of none effect: and the LORD shall forgive her. But every vow of a widow, and of her that is divorced, wherewith they have bound their souls, shall stand against her.

Nu:30:10: *And if she vowed in her husband's house, or bound her soul by a bond with an oath; And her husband heard it, and held his peace at her, and disallowed her not: then all her vows shall stand, and every bond wherewith she bound her soul shall stand. But if her husband hath utterly made them void on the day he heard them; then whatsoever proceeded out of her lips concerning her vows, or concerning the bond of her soul, shall not stand: her husband hath made them void; and the LORD shall forgive her. Every vow, and every binding oath to afflict the soul, her husband may establish it, or her husband may make it void.*

Nu:30:14: *But if her husband altogether hold his peace at her from day to day; then he establisheth all her vows, or all her bonds, which are upon her: he confirmeth them, because he held his peace at her in the day that he heard them. But if he shall any ways make them void after that he hath heard them; then he shall bear her iniquity. These are the statutes, which the LORD commanded Moses, between a man and his wife, between the father and his daughter, being yet in her youth in her father's house.*

(Gen. 31:19-32 *And Laban went to shear his sheep: and Rachel had stolen the images that were her father's. And Jacob stole away unawares to Laban the Syrian, in that he told him not that he fled. So he fled with all that he had; and he rose up, and passed over the river, and set his face toward the mount Gilead. And it was told Laban on the third day that Jacob was fled. And he took his brethren with him, and pursued after him seven days' journey; and they overtook him in the mount Gilead. And God came to Laban the Syrian in a dream by night, and said unto him, Take heed that thou speak not to Jacob either good or bad.*

Then Laban overtook Jacob. Now Jacob had pitched his tent in the mount: and Laban with his brethren pitched in the mount of Gilead.: And Laban said to Jacob, What hast thou done, that thou hast stolen away unawares to me, and carried away my daughters, as captives taken with the sword? Wherefore didst thou flee away secretly, and steal away from me; and didst not tell me, that I might have sent thee away with mirth, and with songs, with tabret, and with harp? And hast not suffered me to kiss my sons and my daughters? thou hast now done foolishly in so doing. It is in the power of my hand to do you hurt: but the God of your father spake unto me yesternight, saying, Take thou heed that thou speak not to Jacob either good or bad.

Gen:31:30: *And now, though thou wouldest needs be gone, because thou sore longedst after thy father's house, yet wherefore hast thou stolen my gods? And Jacob answered and said to Laban, Because I was afraid: for I said,ҳ Peradventure thou wouldest take by force thy daughters from me. With whomsoever thou findest thy gods, let him not live: before our brethren discern thou what is thine with me, and take it to thee. For Jacob knew not that Rachel had stolen them.*

Gen. 31:15-19 *And Jacob called the name of the place where God spake with him, Bethel.*Ge:35:16:*And they journeyed from Bethel; and there was but a* *little way to come to Ephrath: and Rachel travailed, and she had hard labour. And it came to pass, when she was in hard labour, that the midwife said unto her, Fear not; thou shalt have this son also.: And it came to pass, as her soul was in departing, (for she died) that she called his name Ben-oni: but his father called him Benjamin.: And Rachel died, and was buried in the way to Ephrath, which is Bethlehem. E.g (Laban-Jacob-Rachel)*

Case study: 3
The words of evil men can cage you. Is. 25:7 *And he will destroy in this mountain the face of the covering cast over all people, and the vail that is spread over all nations.*

Case study: 4
The words of the prophet can create a disaster in the life of a man. Joshua 9:22-27 *And Joshua called for them, and he spake unto them, saying, Wherefore have ye beguiled us, saying, We are very far from you; when ye dwell among us?: Now therefore ye are cursed, and there shall none of you be freed from being bondmen, and hewers of wood and drawers of water for the house of my God.: And they answered Joshua, and said, Because it was certainly told thy servants, how that the LORD thy God commanded his servant Moses to give you all the land, and to destroy all the inhabitants of the land from before you, therefore we were sore afraid of our lives because of you, and have done this thing. And now, behold, we are in thine hand: as it seemeth good and right unto thee to do unto us, do. Jos:9:26: And so did he unto them, and delivered them out of the hand of the children of Israel, that they slew them not. And Joshua made them that day hewers of wood and drawers of water for the congregation, and for the altar of the LORD, even unto this day, in the place which he should choose.*

1 kings. 13:1-9 And, behold, there came a man of God out of Judah by the word of the LORD unto Bethel: and Jeroboam stood by the altar to burn incense. And he cried against the altar in the word of the LORD, and said, O altar, altar, thus saith the LORD; Behold, a child shall be born unto the house of

David, Josiah by name; and upon thee shall he offer the priests of the high places that burn incense upon thee, and men's bones shall be burnt upon thee. And he gave a sign the same day, saying, This is the sign which the LORD hath spoken; Behold, the altar shall be rent, and the ashes that are upon it shall be poured out. And it came to pass, when king Jeroboam heard the saying of the man of God, which had cried against the altar in Bethel, that he put forth his hand from the altar, saying, Lay hold on him. And his hand, which he put forth against him, dried up, so that he could not pull it in again to him. The altar also was rent, and the ashes poured out from the altar, according to the sign which the man of God had given by the word of the LORD. And the king answered and said unto the man of God, Intreat now the face of the LORD thy God, and pray for me, that my hand may be restored me again. And the man of God besought the LORD, and the king's hand was restored him again, and became as it was before. And the king said unto the man of God, Come home with me, and refresh thyself, and I will give thee a reward. And the man of God said unto the king, If thou wilt give me half thine house, I will not go in with thee, neither will I eat bread nor drink water in this place:

For so was it charged me by the word of the LORD, saying, Eat no bread, nor drink water, nor turn again by the same way that thou camest.

HOW DO I REVERSE NEGATIVE PRONOUNCEMENT?

1. Engage prophetic declaration from the word of God against those negative pronouncements. Isaiah 8:9-10, *Associate yourselves, O ye people, and ye shall be broken in pieces; and give ear, all ye of far countries: gird yourselves, and ye shall be broken in pieces; gird yourselves, and ye shall be broken in pieces.*

Is. 44:24-26 *Thus saith the LORD, thy redeemer, and he that formed thee from the womb, I am the LORD that maketh all things; that stretcheth forth the heavens alone; that spreadeth abroad the earth by myself; That frustrateth the tokens of the liars, and maketh diviners mad; that turneth wise men backward, and maketh their knowledge foolish; That confirmeth the word of his servant, and performeth the counsel of his messengers; that saith to Jerusalem, Thou shalt be inhabited; and to the cities of Judah, Ye shall be built, and I will raise up the decayed places thereof*

The word of the prophetic can operate in three dimensions.

§ **Pronouncement to yourself.**
(Isaiah 33:24) *Thy tacklings are loosed; they could not well strengthen their mast, they could not spread the sail: then is the prey of a great spoil divided; the lame take the prey.*

§ **Pronouncement to your situation.**
(Ezekiel 37:4-12) *Again he said unto me, Prophesy upon these bones, and say unto them, O ye dry bones, hear the word of the LORD. Thus saith the Lord GOD unto these bones; Behold, I will cause breath to enter into you, and ye shall live: And I will lay sinews upon you, and will bring up flesh upon you, and cover you with skin, and put breath in you, and ye shall live; and ye shall know that I am the LORD. So I prophesied as I was commanded: and as I prophesied, there was a noise, and behold a shaking, and the bones came together, bone to his bone.*

And when I beheld, lo, the sinews and the flesh came up upon them, and the skin covered them above: but there was no breath in them. Then said he unto me, Prophesy unto the wind, prophesy, son of man, and say to the wind, Thus saith the Lord GOD; Come from the four winds, O breath, and breathe upon these slain, that they may live. So I prophesied as he commanded me, and the breath came into them, and they lived, and stood up upon their feet, an exceeding great army. Then he said unto me, Son of man, these bones are the whole house of Israel: behold, they say, Our bones are dried, and our hope is lost: we are cut off for our parts. Therefore prophesy and say unto them, Thus saith the Lord GOD; Behold, O my people, I will open your graves, and cause you to come up out of your graves, and bring you into the land of Israel.)

§   **Pronouncement against your enemies.**

(Ezekiel 11:4,13, Therefore prophesy against them, prophesy, O son of man. And the Spirit of the LORD fell upon me, and said unto me, Speak; Thus saith the LORD; Thus have ye said, O house of Israel: for I know the things that come into your mind, every one of them. Eze:11:6: Ye have multiplied your slain in this city, and ye have filled the streets thereof with the slain. Therefore thus saith the Lord GOD; Your slain whom ye have laid in the midst of it, they are the flesh, and this city is the caldron: but I will bring you forth out of the midst of it. Ye have feared the sword; and I will bring a sword upon you, saith the Lord GOD.

Eze:11:9: And I will bring you out of the midst thereof, and deliver you into the hands of strangers, and will execute judgments among you. Ye shall fall by the sword; I will judge you in the border of Israel; and ye shall know that I am the LORD. This city shall not be your caldron, neither shall ye be the flesh in the midst thereof; but I will judge you in the border of Israel: And ye shall know that I am the LORD: for ye have not walked in my statutes, neither executed my judgments, but have done after the manners of the heathen that are round about you. And it came to pass, when I prophesied, that Pelatiah the son of Benaiah died. Then fell I down upon my face, and cried with a loud voice, and said, Ah Lord GOD! wilt thou make a full end of the remnant of Israel?

Ezekiel 13-1-2 *And the word of the LORD came unto me, saying, Son of man, prophesy against the prophets of Israel that prophesy, and say thou unto them that prophesy out of their own hearts, Hear ye the word of the LORD;*

Ezekiel 21:1-3. *And the word of the LORD came unto me, saying, Eze:21:2: Son of man, set thy face toward Jerusalem, and drop thy word toward the holy places, and prophesy against the land of Israel, Eze:21:3: And say to the land of Israel, Thus saith the LORD; Behold, I am against thee, and will draw forth my sword out of his sheath, and will cut off from thee the righteous and the wicked.*

2. Engage the power of the blood of Jesus for total cleansing. **Heb. 9:22** *And almost all things are by the law purged with blood; and without shedding of blood is no remission.*

Heb. 10:22 *Let us draw near with a true heart in full assurance of faith, having our hearts sprinkled from an evil conscience, and our bodies washed with pure water.*

PRAYER POINTS ON:
THE POWER OF A SPOKEN WORD
1. Every word I have spoken against myself negatively, I cancel it by the blood of Jesus.
2. Lord, everything I have said with my mouth that is working against me and my destiny, today I reverse it by the blood.
3. Everything spoken against me, my children, husband, wife and career, that is fighting my destiny, today I revoke it by the blood of Jesus.
4. Every power from the camp of the enemy that is manipulating my thoughts, actions and deliverance, today I set it on fire for total destruction.

5. Anyone around me that depends on enchantment, astrologers, gainsayers, mood seekers to cage my destiny, may the thunder of God strike them dead.

6. Lord, every negative word that has been spoken into my generation that is affecting my destiny, today I reverse it by the blood of Jesus.

7. Today, by the blood of Jesus I decree eternal frustration over every token of evil positioned to monitor my destiny.

8. Lord today, by the blood of Jesus I baptise with madness all agents of darkness that have been hired against my life, career, and destiny.

9. Lord by the fire of the Holy Ghost I return the wickedness of the wicked against them and I turn their counsel into foolishness.

10. Lord, every power that is manipulating my mind contrary to the plan of God for my life, today I renounce it by the blood of Jesus.

11. By the power of the word of God, I speak to my body, everything God has not planted be rooted out in Jesus name.

12. By the power of the word of God, I prophesy into my destiny. Everything that is not working according to the plan of God be corrected supernaturally now, in Jesus name.

13. By the power of the spoken word of God. I speak against the camp of witches oppressing my life and that of my family, Receive instant judgement now in Jesus name.

14. By the power of the spoken word of God, I decree every invisible power standing before me and my greatness be destroyed by the fire of God.

15. By the authority of God's word, I speak to my hands to produce result that will change my story forever.

CHAPTER SEVEN
WITCHCRAFT OPERATIONS

WHAT IS WITCHCRAFT?

It is the invocation of demonic powers to cast a spell and a curse on someone or something through enchantment, manipulation and divination for the purpose of destroying such individual or something.

WHO OPERATES WITCHCRAFT?

Both male and female. A male witch is called wizard and a female witch is called a witch

What does God say about witches?

1. **Don't seek after them. (Lev. 19:31)** *Regard not them that have familiar spirits, neither seek after wizards, to be defiled by them: I am the LORD your God.* **Lev. 20:6** *it will attract God's judgement*

2. *It is an abomination.* **Duet. 18:10-12.** *There shall not be found among you any one that maketh his son or his daughter to pass through the fire, or that useth divination, or an observer of times, or an enchanter, or a witch, Or a charmer, or a consulter with familiar spirits, or a wizard, or a necromancer. For all that do these things are an abomination unto the LORD: and because of these abominations the LORD thy God doth drive them out from before thee.*

How to deal with witchcraft operation?

1. **It must be put to death. Lev.20:27** *A man also or woman that hath a familiar spirit, or that is a wizard, shall surely be put to death: they shall stone them with stones: their blood shall be upon them.*

2. **Must not be allowed to live.** **Ex. 22:18** *Thou shalt not suffer a witch to live.*

3. **You cut them off Micah 5:9, 12** *Thine hand shall be lifted up upon thine adversaries, and all thine enemies shall be cut off. And I will cut off witchcrafts out of thine hand; and thou shalt have no more soothsayers:*

4. **Send them packing. 1 Samuel 28:3-9,** *Now Samuel was dead, and all Israel had lamented him, and buried him in Ramah, even in his own city. And Saul had put away those that had familiar spirits, and the wizards, out of the land. And the Philistines gathered themselves together, and came and pitched in Shunem: and Saul gathered all Israel together, and they pitched in Gilboa. And when Saul saw the host of the Philistines, he was afraid, and his heart greatly trembled. And when Saul enquired of the LORD, the LORD answered him not, neither by dreams nor by Urim, nor by prophets.7: Then said Saul unto his servants, Seek me a woman that hath a familiar spirit, that I may go to her, and enquire of her. And his servants said to him, Behold, there is a woman that hath a familiar spirit at Endor. And Saul disguised himself, and put on other raiment, and he went, and two men with him, and they came to the woman by night: and he said, I pray thee, divine unto me by the familiar spirit, and bring me him up, whom I shall name unto thee. And the woman said unto him, Behold, thou knowest what Saul hath done, how he hath cut off those that have familiar spirits, and the wizards, out of the land: wherefore then layest thou a snare for my life, to cause me to die*

HOW DO THEY OPERATE?
1. WITCHCRAFT OPERATES THROUGH DREAMS
Examples
* Anytime something great is about to happen to you, you see yourself always at the village, (family background forces).
* The spirit of your dead parents appearing to you(generational covenant).
* Specific woman/man appearing in the day of great visitation (monitoring force)
* Seeing snails (slow motion or stagnation)
* Seeing dogs (uncleanness, adultery, fornication)
* Eating in the dream (spiritual weakness, affliction, body weakness, abdominal disorders, menstrual disorder….)
* Someone collecting your money (devourer)
* Someone collecting your certificate (joblessness)
* Something great dropping from your hand always in the dream (short lived or temporary glory.
* Always seeing yourself working without ending (spirit of labour without result)
* Someone calling you in the dream you can't see (confusion,sometimes such call can lead to mental illness or death)
* You saw yourself naked in the dream (shame and ridicule, psychological disorder)
* Someone covering you with a cloth (loss of glory)
* Polluted environment with urine, excreta (spirit of rejection and lack of favour) etc.

2.   THROUGH FAMILIAR SPIRITS
Text. Lev.20:6. *And the soul that turneth after such as have familiar spirits, and after wizards, to go a whoring after them, I will even set my face against that soul, and will cut him off from among his people.*

What are familiar spirits?
·   The spirit of the dead.
·   It involves casting a spell through incantation.
·   It involves the spirit of defilement.
·   It involves operation of demonic mediums and
necromancers. A necromancer is a spell caster that harbours the
ability to raise, or summon the spirit of the dead. They use their
ability to gain absolute control over their enemies' bodies, minds and
souls. Necromancers, also use disease, poisons, spells, to afflict their
target. They can also inflict their captives with the spirit of fear,
fatigue, excruciating pain, and even gain support of others through
the use of enchantments and spell to dominate others.

Familiar spirits can attack your spirit, soul and body. When they
operate, the following can happen:
An individual can get up suddenly and walk away into unknown
destination. Having a re-occurrence of the same calamity
*   Consistent intercourse with Spirit husband.
*   Consistent intercourse with Spirit wife.
*   Seeing another man or woman with your partner in the
dream.
*   Someone lying down in between or beside your partner in
the dream.
*   Using the face of your family members to afflict you.
*   Finding yourself among strange people under the water or a
tree.
*   Always interacting with snakes.
*   Getting married in the dream especially with the
unknown man.

- Giving birth to children in the dream to unknown man.
- Mistaken identity.
- Masquerade fighting you in a dream.
- Never finding favour
- Always singled out for negative things in the midst of many.
- Sitting among dead people
- Always unlucky

How to deal with them.
Understand that your body is the temple of the lord.
(1 Cor. 6:16-20) *What? know ye not that he which is joined to an harlot is one body? for two, saith he, shall be one flesh. But he that is joined unto the Lord is one spirit. Flee fornication. Every sin that a man doeth is without the body; but he that committeth fornication sinneth against his own body. What? know ye not that your body is the temple of the Holy Ghost which is in you, which ye have of God, and ye are not your own? For ye are bought with a price: therefore glorify God in your body, and in your spirit, which are God's.*

Understand that every defilement is subject to destruction.
(1 cor 3:16-17) *Know ye not that ye are the temple of God, and that the Spirit of God dwelleth in you? If any man defile the temple of God, him shall God destroy; for the temple of God is holy, which temple ye are.*

3.   THROUGH FAMILY MEMBERS

Text: **Micah 7:5-8.** *Trust ye not in a friend, put ye not confidence in a guide: keep the doors of thy mouth from her that lieth in thy bosom. For the son dishonoureth the father, the daughter riseth up against her mother, the daughter in law against her mother in law; a man's enemies are the men of his own house. Therefore I will look unto the LORD; I will wait for the God of my salvation:*

my God will hear me. Rejoice not against me, O mine enemy: when I fall, I shall arise; when I sit in darkness, the LORD shall be a light unto me.
(Songs of Solomon 1:6. *Look not upon me, because I am black, because the sun hath looked upon me: my mother's children were angry with me; they made me the keeper of the vineyards; but mine own vineyard have I not kept.*
One of the most difficult enemies to conquer in life is "household" enemy?
This is so because, they know everything about you. Victory may be delayed and sometimes, most people remain perpetually under their bondage (household enemy) till death, except they ask God to rise up and challenge them to death.

How Does Family Members Put You Into Bondage?
Deut. 13:6-11. *If thy brother, the son of thy mother, or thy son, or thy daughter, or the wife of thy bosom, or thy friend, which is as thine own soul, entice thee secretly, saying, Let us go and serve other gods, which thou hast not known, thou, nor thy fathers; Namely, of the gods of the people which are round about you, nigh unto thee, or far off from thee, from the one end of the earth even unto the other end of the earth; Thou shalt not consent unto him, nor hearken unto him; neither shall thine eye pity him, neither shalt thou spare, neither shalt thou conceal him: But thou shalt surely kill him; thine hand shall be first upon him to put him to death, and afterwards the hand of all the people. And thou shalt stone him with stones, that he die; because he hath sought to thrust thee away from the LORD thy God, which brought thee out of the land of Egypt, from the house of bondage. And all Israel shall hear, and fear, and shall do no more any such wickedness as this is among you.*

· **Through influence of demonic practice so that they can strike you.** The influence of household enemies, is principally to kill, afflict and to stagnate your life.

(Songs of solomon 1: 6) *Look not upon me, because I am black, because the sun hath looked upon me: my mother's children were angry with me; they made me the keeper of the vineyards; but mine own vineyard have I not kept.*

4. THROUGH FALSE PROPHETS

Texts: **Deut.13: 1-5.** *Thou shalt surely smite the inhabitants of that city with the edge of the sword, destroying it utterly, and all that is therein, and the cattle thereof, with the edge of the sword.*

Prophets, are divine messagers that communicate the mind of God to men. Unfortunately, many have ordained themselves into the office of a prophet with the aim of re duplicating the acts and wonders of God through corrupted powers. They are false prophets.

WHO ARE FALSE PROPHETS?

1. **These are satanic agents that use demonic powers to produce signs and wonders as though it is God.**

(Rev. 16:13-14) *And I saw three unclean spirits like frogs come out of the mouth of the dragon, and out of the mouth of the beast, and out of the mouth of the false prophet.Re:16:14: For they are the spirits of devils, working miracles, which go forth unto the kings of the earth and of the whole world, to gather them to the battle of that great day of God Almighty.*

2. **They engage in lying wonders and deception. (2 Thes 2:8-10)** *And then shall that Wicked be revealed, whom the Lord shall consume with the spirit of his mouth, and shall destroy with the brightness of his coming:*

3. **They lead people into errors. Is. 9:14-17** *Therefore the LORD will cut off from Israel head and tail, branch and rush, in one day.Isa:9:15: The ancient and honourable, he is the head; and the prophet that teacheth lies, he is the tail. For the leaders of this people cause them to err; and they that are led of them are destroyed.*

Therefore the Lord shall have no joy in their young men, neither shall have mercy on their fatherless and widows: for everyone is an hypocrite and an evildoer, and every mouth speaketh folly. For all this his anger is not turned away, but his hand is stretched out still.

4. They prophesy lies. (JER. 14:.13.15) *Take the girdle that thou hast got, which is upon thy loins, and arise, go to Euphrates, and hide it there in a hole of the rock. So I went, and hid it by Euphrates, as the LORD commanded me. And it came to pass after many days, that the LORD said unto me, Arise, go to Euphrates, and take the girdle from thence, which I commanded thee to hide there. Then I went to Euphrates, and digged, and took the girdle from the place where I had hid it: and, behold, the girdle was marred, it was profitable for nothing. Then the word of the LORD came unto me, saying, Thus saith the LORD, After this manner will I mar the pride of Judah, and the great pride of Jerusalem. This evil people, which refuse to hear my words, which walk in the imagination of their heart, and walk after other gods, to serve them, and to worship them, shall even be as this girdle, which is good for nothing. For as the girdle cleaveth to the loins of a man, so have I caused to cleave unto me the whole house of Israel and the whole house of Judah, saith the LORD; that they might be unto me for a people, and for a name, and for a praise, and for a glory: but they would not hear. Therefore thou shalt speak unto them this word; Thus saith the LORD God of Israel, Every bottle shall be filled with wine: and they shall say unto thee, Do we not certainly know that every bottle shall be filled with wine? Then shalt thou say unto them, Thus saith the LORD, Behold, I will fill all the inhabitants of this land, even the kings that sit upon David's throne, and the priests, and the prophets, and all the inhabitants of Jerusalem, with drunkenness. And I will dash them one against another, even the fathers and the sons together, saith the LORD: I will not pity, nor spare, nor have mercy, but destroy them. Hear ye, and give ear; be not proud: for the LORD hath spoken.*

5. **They see false visions. (Ezekiel 13:1-9)** *And the word of the LORD came unto me, saying, Son of man, prophesy against the prophets of Israel that prophesy, and say thou unto them that prophesy out of their own hearts, Hear ye the word of the LORD; Thus saith the Lord GOD; Woe unto the foolish prophets, that follow their own spirit, and have seen nothing! O Israel, thy prophets are like the foxes in the deserts. Ye have not gone up into the gaps, neither made up the hedge for the house of Israel to stand in the battle in the day of the LORD. They have seen vanity and lying divination, saying, The LORD saith: and the LORD hath not sent them: and they have made others to hope that they would confirm the word. Have ye not seen a vain vision, and have ye not spoken a lying divination, whereas ye say, The LORD saith it; albeit I have not spoken? Therefore thus saith the Lord GOD; Because ye have spoken vanity, and seen lies, therefore, behold, I am against you, saith the Lord GOD. And mine hand shall be upon the prophets that see vanity, and that divine lies: they shall not be in the assembly of my people, neither shall they be written in the writing of the house of Israel, neither shall they enter into the land of Israel; and ye shall know that I am the Lord GOD.*

6. **They operate with witchcraft network. Ezekiel. 31:17-23** *Likewise, thou son of man, set thy face against the daughters of thy people, which prophesy out of their own heart; and prophesy thou against them, And say, Thus saith the Lord GOD; Woe to the women that sew pillows to all armholes, and make kerchiefs upon the head of every stature to hunt souls! Will ye hunt the souls of my people, and will ye save the souls alive that come unto you? And will ye pollute me among my people for handfuls of barley and for pieces of bread, to slay the souls that should not die, and to save the souls alive that should not live, by your lying to my people that hear your lies? Wherefore thus saith the Lord GOD; Behold, I am against your pillows, wherewith ye there hunt the souls to make them fly, and I will tear them from your arms, and will let the souls go, even the souls that ye hunt to make them fly. Your kerchiefs also will I tear, and deliver my people*

out of your hand, and they shall be no more in your hand to be hunted; and ye shall know that I am the LORD. Because with lies ye have made the heart of the righteous sad, whom I have not made sad; and strengthened the hands of the wicked, that he should not return from his wicked way, *by promising him life: Therefore ye shall see no more vanity, nor divine divinations: for I will deliver my people out of your hand: and ye shall know that I am the LORD.*

THE WEAKNESSES OF FALSE PROPHETS

1. Their visions, miracles do not stand the test of time.
2. Most times they see troubles, but they hardly produce permanent solutions to the troubles.
3. Most times, what you receive from them multiplies your troubles.

(Number 5:11-13) *And the LORD spake unto Moses, saying, Speak unto the children of Israel, and say unto them, If any man's wife go aside, and commit a trespass against him, And a man lie with her carnally, and it be hid from the eyes of her husband, and be kept close, and she be defiled, and there be no witness against her, neither she be taken with the manner; And the spirit of jealousy come upon him, and he be jealous of his wife, and she be defiled: or if the spirit of jealousy come upon him, and he be jealous of his wife, and she be not defiled Then shall the man bring his wife unto the priest, and he shall bring her offering for her, the tenth part of an ephah of barley meal; he shall pour no oil upon it, nor put frankincense thereon; for it is an offering of jealousy, an offering of memorial, bringing iniquity to remembrance. And the priest shall bring her near, and set her before the LORD: And the priest shall take holy water in an earthen vessel; and of the dust that is in the floor of the tabernacle the priest shall take, and put it into the water: And the priest shall set the woman before the LORD, and uncover the woman's head, and put the offering of memorial in her hands, which is the jealousy offering: and the priest shall have in his hand the bitter water that causeth the curse: And the priest shall charge her by an oath, and say unto the woman, If* *no man have lain with thee, and if thou hast not gone aside to uncleanness with another instead of thy husband, be thou free from this bitter water that causeth the curse: But if thou hast gone aside to another instead of thy husband, and if thou be defiled, and some man have lain with thee beside thine husband: Then the priest shall charge the woman with an oath of cursing, and the priest shall say unto the woman, The LORD make thee a curse and an oath among thy people, when the LORD doth make thy thigh to rot, and thy belly to swell; And this water that causeth the curse shall go into thy bowels, to make thy belly to swell, and thy thigh to rot: And the woman shall say, Amen, amen. And the priest shall write these curses in a book, and he shall blot them out with the bitter water: And he shall cause the woman to drink the bitter water that causeth the curse: and the water that causeth the curse shall enter into her, and become bitter. Then the priest shall take the jealousy offering out of the woman's hand, and shall wave the offering before the LORD, and offer it upon the altar: And the priest shall take an handful of the offering, even the memorial thereof, and burn it upon the altar, and afterward shall cause the woman to drink the water. And when he hath made her to drink the water, then it shall come to pass, that, if she be defiled, and have done trespass against her husband, that the water that causeth the curse shall enter into her, and become bitter, and her belly shall swell, and her thigh shall rot: and the woman shall be a curse among her people. And if the woman be not defiled, but be clean; then she shall be free, and shall conceive seed. This is the law of jealousies, when a wife goeth aside to another instead of her husband, and is defiled; or when the spirit of jealousy cometh upon him, and he be jealous over his wife, and shall set the woman before the LORD, and the priest shall execute upon her all this law. Then shall the man be guiltless from iniquity, and this woman shall bear her iniquity.*

HOW TO HANDLE THE FALSE PROPHET

A. Invoke God against their powers.

1s. 47:1-15 *Stand now with thine enchantments, and with the multitude of thy sorceries, wherein thou hast laboured from thy youth; if so be thou shalt be able to profit, if so be thou mayest prevail. Thou art wearied in the multitude of thy counsels. Let now the astrologers, the stargazers, the monthly* *prognosticators, stand up, and save thee from these things that shall come upon thee. Behold, they shall be as stubble; the fire shall burn them; they shall not deliver themselves from the power of the flame: there shall not be a coal to warm at, nor fire to sit before it. Thus shall they be unto thee with whom thou hast laboured, even thy merchants, from thy youth: they shall wander every one to his quarter; none shall save thee.*

B. Revoke all negative pronouncement.

Is. 8:9 *Associate yourselves, O ye people, and ye shall be broken in pieces; and give ear, all ye of far countries: gird yourselves, and ye shall be broken in pieces; gird yourselves, and ye shall be broken in pieces Take counsel together, and it shall come to nought; speak the word, and it shall not stand: for God is with us.*

C. Don't follow or practise any of their ways.

Is. 8:11,19 *For the LORD spake thus to me with a strong hand, and instructed me that I should not walk in the way of this people, saying, And when they shall say unto you, Seek unto them that have familiar spirits, and unto wizards that peep, and that mutter: should not a people seek unto their God? for the living to the dead?*

5. THROUGH CULTURAL AFFLICTION

Text: **Num. 5:11-31** *And the LORD spake unto Moses, saying, Speak unto the children of Israel, and say unto them, If any man's wife go aside, and commit a trespass against him, And a man lie with her carnally, and it be hid from the eyes of her husband, and be kept close, and she be defiled, and there be no witness against her, neither she be taken with the manner; And the spirit of jealousy come upon him, and he be jealous of his wife, and she be defiled: or if the spirit of jealousy come upon him, and he be jealous of his wife, and she be not defiled: Then shall the man bring his wife unto the priest, and he shall bring her offering for her, the tenth part of an ephah of barley meal; he shall pour no oil upon it, nor put frankincense thereon; for it is an offering of jealousy, an offering of memorial,* *bringing iniquity to remembrance. And the priest shall bring her near, and set her before the LORD: And the priest shall take holy water in an earthen vessel; and of the dust that is in the floor of the tabernacle the priest shall take, and put it into the water: And the priest shall set the woman before the LORD, and uncover the woman's head, and put the offering of memorial in her hands, which is the jealousy offering: and the priest shall have in his hand the bitter water that causeth the curse: And the priest shall charge her by an oath, and say unto the woman, If no man have lain with thee, and if thou hast not gone aside to uncleanness with another instead of thy husband, be thou free from this bitter water that causeth the curse: But if thou hast gone aside to another instead of thy husband, and if thou be defiled, and some man have lain with thee beside thine husband: Then the priest shall charge the woman with an oath of cursing, and the priest shall say unto the woman, The LORD make thee a curse and an oath among thy people, when the LORD doth make thy thigh to rot, and thy belly to swell; And this water that causeth the curse shall go into thy bowels, to make thy belly to swell, and thy thigh to rot: And the woman shall say, Amen, amen. And the priest shall write these curses in a book, and he shall blot them out with the bitter water: And he shall cause the woman to drink the bitter water that causeth the curse: and the water that causeth the curse shall enter into her, and become bitter. Then the priest shall take the jealousy offering out of the woman's hand, and shall wave the offering before the LORD, and offer it upon the altar: And the priest shall take an handful of the offering, even the memorial thereof, and burn it upon the altar, and afterward shall cause the woman to drink the water. And when he hath made her to drink the water, then it shall come to pass, that, if she be defiled, and have done trespass against her husband, that the water that causeth the curse shall enter into her, and become bitter, and her belly shall swell, and her thigh shall rot: and the woman shall be a curse among her people. And if the woman be not defiled, but be clean; then she shall be free, and shall conceive seed. This is the law of jealousies, when a wife goeth aside to another instead of her husband, and is defiled; Or when the spirit of jealousy cometh upon him, and he be jealous over his wife, and shall set the woman before the LORD, and the priest shall execute upon her all this law. Then shall the man be guiltless from iniquity, and this woman shall bear her iniquity.*

WHAT ARE CULTURAL AFFLICTIONS?

They are demonic attacks that are inflicted on individuals through unclean cultural practices.

Case study. (A)

A.   An oath by a woman at the obituary site over the dead of her husband.

B.   Covenant with the forces of the land on a given gender:

* When you marry their girls who are beautiful like queens, but life becomes miserable, because all their females have been covenanted to the deities of the land.

* Male of a given community who does not live beyond 50years. Hence, their women become widows at young age.

C.   The spirit of your deities appearing every time you are set for a change of story.

D.   Food offered to Idols. E.g. someone ate the food offered to idols, and developed a swollen tummy that defiles medication and end up killing the individual.

E.   Bathing with satanic soap. A woman decided to bathe with a soup that has been enchanted upon by a witch priest for the purpose of regaining her husband back from the hands of strange women. Unfortunately, after the bath, the husband set his eyes on her, but developed an irrevocable hatred leading to his exit from his matrimonial home to stay permanently with a strange woman.

F.   Bathing in the river for conception purpose. This can lead to giving birth to children that trouble the family in the future.

H.   Re-occurrence of a sickness in a family at a particular month, until a given sacrifice is done, or has developed into a cultural affliction.

How to Handle Cultural Affliction

A. **Raise an altar of prayer through the blood of Jesus to purge you of all inherited or deliberate act with satanic covenant. Col.2:14-15** *Blotting out the handwriting of ordinances that was against us, which was contrary to us, and took it out of the way, nailing it to his cross; And having spoiled principalities and powers, he made a shew of them openly, triumphing over them in it.*

B. **Raise an altar of sacrifice before God, as led by Him to terminate the root of such affliction in your life.**
2 Sam. 24:15-25 *So the LORD sent a pestilence upon Israel from the morning even to the time appointed: and there died of the people from Dan even to Beer-sheba seventy thousand men. And when the angel stretched out his hand upon Jerusalem to destroy it, the LORD repented him of the evil, and said to the angel that destroyed the people, It is enough: stay now thine hand. And the angel of the LORD was by the threshingplace of Araunah the Jebusite. And David spake unto the LORD when he saw the angel that smote the people, and said, Lord, I have sinned, and I have done wickedly: but these sheep, what have they done? let thine hand, I pray thee, be against me, and against my father's house. And Gad came that day to David, and said unto him, Go up, rear an altar unto the LORD in the threshingfloor of Araunah the Jebusite. And David, according to the saying of Gad, went up as the LORD commanded. And Araunah looked, and saw the king and his servants coming on toward him: and Araunah went out, and bowed himself before the king on his face upon the ground. And Araunah said, Wherefore is my lord the king come to his servant? And David said, To buy the threshing floor of thee, to build an altar unto the LORD, that the plague may be stayed from the people. And Araunah said unto David, Let my lord the king take and offer up what seemeth good unto him: behold, here be oxen for burnt sacrifice, and threshing instruments and other instruments of the*

oxen for wood. All these things did Araunah, as a king, give unto the king. And Araunah said unto the king, The LORD thy God accept thee. And the king said unto Araunah, Nay; but I will surely buy it of thee at a price: neither will I offer burnt offerings unto the LORD my God of that which doth cost me nothing. So David bought the threshingfloor and the oxen for fifty shekels of silver. And David built there an altar unto the LORD, and offered burnt offerings and peace offerings. So the LORD was intreated for the land, and the plague was stayed from Israel.

6   THROUGH SPIRITUAL SHADOWS

Spiritual shadows are the manifestations of devils through symbolic objects and strange sounds. **(Daniel 5:1-31)** *Belshazzar the king made a great feast to a thousand of his lords, and drank wine before the thousand. Belshazzar, whiles he tasted the wine, commanded to bring the golden and silver vessels which his father Nebuchadnezzar had taken out of the temple which was in Jerusalem; that the king, and his princes, his wives, and his concubines, might drink therein. Then they brought the golden vessels that were taken out of the temple of the house of God which was at Jerusalem; and the king, and his princes, his wives, and his concubines, drank in them. They drank wine, and praised the gods of gold, and of silver, of brass, of iron, of wood, and of stone. In the same hour came forth fingers of a man's hand, and wrote over against the candlestick upon the plaister of the wall of the king's palace: and the king saw the part of the hand that wrote. Then the king's countenance was changed, and his thoughts troubled him, so that the joints of his loins were loosed, and his knees smote one against another. The king cried aloud to bring in the astrologers, the Chaldeans, and the soothsayers. And the king spake, and said to the wise men of Babylon, Whosoever shall read this writing, and shew me the interpretation thereof, shall be clothed with scarlet, and have a chain of gold about his neck, and shall be the third ruler in the kingdom. Then came in all the king's wise men: but they could not read the writing, nor make known to the king the interpretation thereof. Then was king Belshazzar greatly troubled, and his countenance was changed in him, and his lords were astonied. Now the queen, by reason of the words of the king* *and his lords, came into the banquet house: and the queen spake and said, O king, live for ever: let not thy thoughts trouble thee, nor let thy countenance be changed: There is a man in thy kingdom, in whom is the spirit of the holy gods; and in the days of thy father light and understanding and wisdom, like the wisdom of the gods, was found in him; whom the king Nebuchadnezzar thy father, the king, I say, thy father, made master of the magicians, astrologers, Chaldeans, and soothsayers; Forasmuch as an excellent spirit, and knowledge, and understanding, interpreting of dreams, and shewing of hard sentences, and dissolving of doubts, were found in the same Daniel, whom the king named Belteshazzar: now let Daniel be called, and he will shew the interpretation. Then was Daniel brought in before the king. And the king spake and said unto Daniel, Art thou that Daniel, which art of the children of the captivity of Judah, whom the king my father brought out of Jewry? I have even heard of thee, that the spirit of the gods is in thee, and that light and understanding and excellent wisdom is found in thee. And now the wise men, the astrologers, have been brought in before me, that they should read this writing, and make known unto me the interpretation thereof: but they could not shew the interpretation of the thing: And I have heard of thee, that thou canst make interpretations, and dissolve doubts: now if thou canst read the writing, and make known to me the interpretation thereof, thou shalt be clothed with scarlet, and have a chain of gold about thy neck, and shalt be the third ruler in the kingdom. Then Daniel answered and said before the king, Let thy gifts be to thyself, and give thy rewards to another; yet I will read the writing unto the king, and make known to him the interpretation. O thou king, the most high God gave Nebuchadnezzar thy father a kingdom, and majesty, and glory, and honour: And for the majesty that he gave him, all people, nations, and languages, trembled and feared before him: whom he would he slew; and whom he would he kept alive; and whom he would he set up; and whom he would he put down. But when his heart was lifted up, and his mind hardened in pride, he was deposed from his kingly throne, and they took his glory from him: And he was driven from the sons of men; and his heart was made like the beasts, and his dwelling was with the wild asses: they fed him with grass like oxen, and his body was wet with the dew of heaven; till he knew that the most high*

God ruled in the kingdom of men, and that he appointeth over it whomsoever he will. And thou his son, O Belshazzar, hast not humbled thine heart, though thou knewest all this; But hast lifted up thyself against the LORD of heaven; and they have brought the vessels of his house before thee, and thou, and thy lords, thy wives, and thy concubines, have drunk wine in them; and thou hast praised the gods of silver, and gold, of brass, iron, wood, and stone, which see not, nor hear, nor know: and the God in whose hand thy breath is, and whose are all thy ways, hast thou not glorified: Then was the part of the hand sent from him; and this writing was written. And this is the writing that was written, MENE, MENE, TEKEL, UPHARSIN. This is the interpretation of the thing: MENE; God hath numbered thy kingdom, and finished it. TEKEL; Thou art weighed in the balances, and art found wanting. PERES; Thy kingdom is divided, and given to the Medes and Persians. Then commanded Belshazzar, and they clothed Daniel with scarlet, and put a chain of gold about his neck, and made a proclamation concerning him, that he should be the third ruler in the kingdom. In that night was Belshazzar the king of the Chaldeans slain. And Darius the Median took the kingdom, being about threescore and two years old.

Examples:
- Hearing strange voices talking to you.
- Someone calling your name which cannot be traced.
- Invisible hand slapping you.
- Invisible being walking on the wall of your house.
- Sudden disappearance of things which look very impossible.
- Invisible cobwebs covering your face.
- Interacting with the appearance of strange beings that only you can see.
- Living the opposite of life that looks real to you.

(Act. 8:9-13) *But there was a certain man, called Simon, which before time in the same city used sorcery, and bewitched the people of Samaria, giving out that himself was some great one: To whom they all gave heed, from the least to the* *greatest, saying, This man is the great power of God. And to him they had regard, because that of long time he had bewitched them with sorceries. But when they believed Philip preaching the things concerning the kingdom of God, and the name of Jesus Christ, they were baptized, both men and women. Then Simon himself believed also: and when he was baptized, he continued with Philip, and wondered, beholding the miracles and signs which were done..(18-24) And when Simon saw that through laying on of the apostles' hands the Holy Ghost was given, he offered them money, Saying, Give me also this power, that on whomsoever I lay hands, he may receive the Holy Ghost. But Peter said unto him, Thy money perish with thee, because thou hast thought that the gift of God may be purchased with money. Thou hast neither part nor lot in this matter: for thy heart is not right in the sight of God. Repent therefore of this thy wickedness, and pray God, if perhaps the thought of thine heart may be forgiven thee. For I perceive that thou art in the gall of bitterness, and in the bond of iniquity. Then answered Simon, and said, Pray ye to the Lord for me, that none of these things which ye have spoken come upon me.*

HOW TO HANDLE SPIRITUAL SHADOWS

A. Invoke the power of the Holy Ghost against the appearances of those strange beings as contained in the above scriptures.

B. Invoke the mystery of the blood of Jesus in prayers and sprinkle yourself and your environment with the blood

Heb. 9:20-22 *Saying, This is the blood of the testament which God hath enjoined unto you. Moreover he sprinkled with blood both the tabernacle, and all the vessels of the ministry. And almost all things are by the law purged with blood; and without shedding of blood is no remission.*

Heb. 11:28 *Through faith he kept the passover, and the sprinkling of blood, lest he that destroyed the firstborn should touch them.*

7.   THROUGH CIRCUMSTANCIAL NAMES FROM THE DEVIL.

A. VISIBLE LIFE CASES

Life cases that have made some people's names to be forgotten. The society refers to them by their situation that has come to be their popular name.

Example1 (the woman with the issue of blood)

Mark. 5:25-34. *And a certain woman, which had an issue of blood twelve years, And had suffered many things of many physicians, and had spent all that she had, and was nothing bettered, but rather grew worse, When she had heard of Jesus, came in the press behind, and touched his garment. For she said, If I may touch but his clothes, I shall be whole. And straightway the fountain of her blood was dried up; and she felt in her body that she was healed of that plague. And Jesus, immediately knowing in himself that virtue had gone out of him, turned him about in the press, and said, Who touched my clothes? And his disciples said unto him, Thou seest the multitude thronging thee, and sayest thou, Who touched me? And he looked round about to see her that had done this thing. But the woman fearing and trembling, knowing what was done in her, came and fell down before him, and told him all the truth. And he said unto her, Daughter, thy faith hath made thee whole; go in peace, and be whole of thy plague.*

Example.2 (the Samaritan woman)

Jn. 4:6-18 *Now Jacob's well was there. Jesus therefore, being wearied with his journey, sat thus on the well: and it was about the sixth hour. There cometh a woman of Samaria to draw water: Jesus saith unto her, Give me to drink. (For his disciples were gone away unto the city to buy meat.) Then saith the woman of Samaria unto him, How is it that thou, being a Jew, askest drink of me, which am a woman of Samaria? for the Jews have no dealings with the Samaritans. Jesus answered and said unto her, If thou knewest the gift of God, and who it is that saith to thee, Give me to drink; thou wouldest have asked of him, and he would have given thee living water. The woman saith unto him, Sir, thou hast nothing to draw with, and the well is deep: from whence then hast thou that living water? Art thou greater than our father Jacob, which gave us the well, and drank thereof himself, and his children, and his cattle? Jesus answered and said unto her, Whosoever drinketh of this water shall thirst again: But whosoever drinketh of the water that I shall give him shall never thirst; but the water that I shall give him shall be in him a well of water springing up into everlasting life. The woman saith unto him, Sir, give me this water, that I thirst not, neither come hither to draw. Jesus saith unto her, Go, call thy husband, and come hither*

INVISIBLE LIFE CASES.

These are life experiences that are abnormal, but appear real to the individual because it is being controlled purely from the realm of the spirit. For instance, a child hearing a strange voice asking him to steal and he obeys consistently, can attract a name as a result of the circumstance in his life.

Zech.3:1-10) *And he shewed me Joshua the high priest standing before the angel of the LORD, and Satan standing at his right hand to resist him. And the LORD said unto Satan, The LORD rebuke thee, O Satan; even the LORD that hath chosen Jerusalem rebuke thee: is not this a brand plucked out of the fire? Now Joshua was clothed with filthy garments, and stood before the angel. And he answered and spake unto those that stood before him, saying, Take away the filthy garments from him. And unto him he said, Behold, I have caused thine iniquity to pass from thee, and I will clothe thee with change of raiment. And I said, Let them set a fair mitre upon his head. So they set a fair mitre upon his head, and clothed him with garments. And the angel of the LORD stood by. And the angel of the LORD protested unto Joshua, saying, Thus saith the LORD of hosts; If thou wilt walk in my ways, and if thou wilt keep my charge, then thou shalt also judge my house, and shalt also keep my courts, and I will give thee places to walk among these that stand by. Hear now, O Joshua the high priest, thou, and thy fellows that sit before thee: for they are men wondered at: for, behold, I will bring forth my servant the BRANCH.*

For behold the stone that I have laid before Joshua; upon one stone shall be seven eyes: behold, I will engrave the graving thereof, saith the LORD of hosts, and I will remove the iniquity of that land in one day. In that day, saith the LORD of hosts, shall ye call every man his neighbour under the vine and under the fig tree.

HOW TO HANDLE IT.

A.   Ask God for a permanent change of the circumstances around you.

1 Chro. 4:9-10 *And Jabez was more honourable than his brethren: and his mother called his name Jabez, saying, Because I bare him with sorrow. And Jabez called on the God of Israel, saying, Oh that thou wouldest bless me indeed, and enlarge my coast, and that thine hand might be with me, and that thou wouldest keep me from evil, that it may not grieve me! And God granted him that which he requested.*

B.   Ask God to remove all veils covering your eyes.

Is. 25:7-9 *And he will destroy in this mountain the face of the covering cast over all people, and the vail that is spread over all nations. He will swallow up death in victory; and the Lord GOD will wipe away tears from off all faces; and the rebuke of his people shall he take away from off all the earth: for the LORD hath spoken it. And it shall be said in that day, Lo, this is our God; we have waited for him, and he will save us: this is the LORD; we have waited for him, we will be glad and rejoice in his salvation.*

8.   THROUGH MANIPULATION

WHAT IS MANIPULATION?

1. It is a demonic spirit cast upon a man to do things contrary to his will.

   Case study 1.

   A man collecting his salary and giving it to ritualist and fraudsters on a monthly basis.

2. It is an unclean spirit that influences the helper of a man into trouble so as not to help him/her.

Case study 2

A lady observed that anytime she takes a man home to be introduced to get married, that is when calamity happens to the man and his family.

3. It is a spiritual force that keeps a man on one spot and blindfolds his mind not to think about advancement in life.

Case study 3

Reading through the works of a great man of God in this country, I found this relevant story stated below:
"In a prayer conference, a prayer point was raised; Lord, every strong man at the gate of my promised land be destroyed, fall and die.

She fell down, saw herself in front of a great king, and the man responded, "Welcome, the sixth wife." She rejected it and repeated the prayer. THE GREAT KING fell down and she looked. Behold, it was her five sisters that were not married, that were surrounding the man. She and her five sisters were finally delivered after an intense spiritual battle in the realm of the spirit".

4.   It is a spirit of strange stubbornness that does not allow a man to take counsel that will better his life until he's destroyed.

Case study 4

A student was brought for prayers and her mother came with him. He was looking like an HIV/AIDS carrier, very lean. He was confirmed not to have any virus of HIV/AIDS. He confessed that one day, he met a sister on campus and he made sure he had sex with her, contrary to the moral counsel he received.

When they finished the immorality, she dipped a piece of cotton wool into her private part, and sucked out his semen (sperm). Before he knew it, she had left the room with the cotton wool. He never saw the girl again and right from that day, he started getting lean.

5.	It is a monitoring spirit that controls the will and thoughts of a man towards his destiny.

Case study 5

One day, a man entered into his room and packed his belongings into a travelling bag, carried the bag and said his goodbye.

The wife asked where he was going and she tried to hold him back. He overpowered her and left. She fell and started crying. Suddenly the Holy Spirit told her to start praying instead of crying. She went and picked her prayer note and began to pray vigorously. Suddenly she looked up and saw a wall-gecko on the wall staring at her. She tried to scare it off, but it would not move. She threw something at it and it fell and ran towards her and bite her toe. She got angry and made sure she caught it and smashed it to death. She poured anointing oil on it and burnt it. As the first smoke from it was dissipating into the thin air, she heard a voice of her husband at the gate—a very serious matter.

Biblical proofs of manipulation.

2sam 24:1-3 (David) *and again the anger of the LORD was kindled against Israel, and he moved David against them to say, Go, number Israel and Judah. For the king said to Joab the captain of the host, which was with him, Go now through all the tribes of Israel, from Dan even to Beer-sheba, and number ye the people, that I may know the number of the people. And Joab said unto the king, Now the LORD thy God add unto the people, how many soever they be, an hundredfold, and that the eyes of my lord the king may see it: but why doth my lord the king delight in this thing?*

Luke 15:11-32 *And when they had brought their ships to land, they forsook all, and followed him. And it came to pass, when he was in a certain city, behold a man* *full of leprosy: who seeing Jesus fell on his face, and besought him, saying, Lord, if thou wilt, thou canst make me clean. And he put forth his hand, and touched him, saying, I will: be thou clean. And immediately the leprosy departed from him. And he charged him to tell no man: but go, and shew thyself to the priest, and offer for thy cleansing, according as Moses commanded, for a testimony unto them. But so much the more went there a fame abroad of him: and great multitudes came together to hear, and to be healed by him of their infirmities. And he withdrew himself into the wilderness, and prayed. And it came to pass on a certain day, as he was teaching, that there were Pharisees and doctors of the law sitting by, which were come out of every town of Galilee, and Judaea, and Jerusalem: and the power of the Lord was present to heal them. And, behold, men brought in a bed a man which was taken with a palsy: and they sought means to bring him in, and to lay him before him. And when they could not find by what way they might bring him in because of the multitude, they went upon the housetop, and let him down through the tiling with his couch into the midst before Jesus. And when he saw their faith, he said unto him, Man, thy sins are forgiven thee. And the scribes and the Pharisees began to reason, saying, Who is this which speaketh blasphemies? Who can forgive sins, but God alone? But when Jesus perceived their thoughts, he answering said unto them, What reason ye in your hearts? Whether is easier, to say, Thy sins be forgiven thee; or to say, Rise up and walk? But that ye may know that the Son of man hath power upon earth to forgive sins, (he said unto the sick of the palsy,) I say unto thee, Arise, and take up thy couch, and go into thine house. And immediately he rose up before them, and took up that whereon he lay, and departed to his own house, glorifying God. And they were all amazed, and they glorified God, and were filled with fear, saying, We have seen strange things to day. And after these things he went forth, and saw a publican, named Levi, sitting at the receipt of custom: and he said unto him, Follow me. And he left all, rose up, and followed him. And Levi made him a great feast in his own house: and there was a great company of publicans and of others that sat down with them. But their scribes and Pharisees murmured against his disciples, saying, Why do ye eat and drink with publicans and sinners? And Jesus answering said unto them, They that are whole need not a physician; but they that are sick. I came not to call the righteous, but sinners to repentance. (Prodigal son)*

HOW TO HANDLE THEM
·   **Terminate every wind of manipulation around you.**
Jere. 4:11 At that time shall it be said to this people and to Jerusalem, A dry wind of the high places in the wilderness toward the daughter of my people, not to fan, nor to cleanse.

·   **Return the arrow back to where they came from.**

Isaiah 37:33-36 *Therefore thus saith the LORD concerning the king of Assyria, He shall not come into this city, nor shoot an arrow there nor come before it with shields, nor cast a bank against it. By the way that he came, by the same shall he return, and shall not come into this city, saith the LORD. For I will defend this city to save it for mine own sake, and for my servant David's sake. Then the angel of the LORD went forth, and smote in the camp of the Assyrians a hundred and fourscore and five thousand: and when they arose early in the morning, behold, they were all dead corpses*

·   **position the wild wind against them.**
Jeremiah. 30:22-24 *And ye shall be my people, and I will be your God. Behold, the whirlwind of the LORD goeth forth with fury, a continuing whirlwind: it shall fall with pain upon the head of the wicked. The fierce anger of the LORD shall not return, until he have done it, and until he have performed the intents of his heart: in the latter days ye shall consider it.*

9.   THROUGH DEMONIC SACRIFICE OVER THE LAND WHERE YOU DWELL
Text: 2king 2:18-22, *and when they came again to him, (for he tarried at Jericho,) he said unto them, Did I not say unto you, Go not? And the men of the city said unto Elisha, Behold, I pray thee, the situation of this city is pleasant, as*

my lord seeth: but the water is naught, and the ground barren. And he said, Bring me a new cruse, and put salt therein. And they brought it to him. And he went forth unto the spring of the waters, and cast the salt in there, and said, Thus saith the LORD, I have healed these waters; there shall not be from thence any more death or barren land. So the waters were healed unto this day, according to the saying of Elisha which he spake.

Num.13:27-33, *And they told him, and said, We came unto the land whither thou sentest us, and surely it floweth with milk and honey; and this is the fruit of it. Nevertheless the people be strong that dwell in the land, and the cities are walled, and very great: and moreover we saw the children of Anak there. The Amalekites dwell in the land of the south: and the Hittites, and the Jebusites, and the Amorites, dwell in the mountains: and the Canaanites dwell by the sea, and by the coast of Jordan. And Caleb stilled the people before Moses, and said, Let us go up at once, and possess it; for we are well able to overcome it. But the men that went up with him said, We be not able to go up against the people; for they are stronger than we. And they brought up an evil report of the land which they had searched unto the children of Israel, saying, The land, through which we have gone to search it, is a land that eateth up the inhabitants thereof; and all the people that we saw in it are men of a great stature. And there we saw the giants, the sons of Anak, which come of the giants: and we were in our own sight as grasshoppers, and so we were in their sight.*

Num14:7-24. *And they spake unto all the company of the children of Israel, saying, The land, which we passed through to search it, is an exceeding good land. If the LORD delight in us, then he will bring us into this land, and give it us; a land which floweth with milk and honey. Only rebel not ye against the LORD, neither fear ye the people of the land; for they are bread for us: their defence is departed from them, and the LORD is with us: fear them not. But all the congregation bade stone them with stones. And the glory of the LORD appeared in the tabernacle of the congregation before all the children of Israel. And the LORD said unto Moses, How long will this people provoke me? and how long* *will it be ere they believe me, for all the signs which I have shewed among them? I will smite them with the pestilence, and disinherit them, and will make of thee a greater nation and mightier than they. And Moses said unto the LORD, Then the Egyptians shall hear it, (for thou broughtest up this people in thy might from among them;) And they will tell it to the inhabitants of this land: for they have heard that thou LORD art among this people, that thou LORD art seen face to face, and that thy cloud standeth over them, and that thou goest before them, by day time in a pillar of a cloud, and in a pillar of fire by night. Now if thou shalt kill all this people as one man, then the nations which have heard the fame of thee will speak, saying,: Because the LORD was not able to bring this people into the land which he sware unto them, therefore he hath slain them in the wilderness. And now, I beseech thee, let the power of my Lord be great, according as thou hast spoken, saying, The LORD is longsuffering, and of great mercy, forgiving iniquity and transgression, and by no means clearing the guilty, visiting the iniquity of the fathers upon the children unto the third and fourth generation. Pardon, I beseech thee, the iniquity of this people according unto the greatness of thy mercy, and as thou hast forgiven this people, from Egypt even until now. And the LORD said, I have pardoned according to thy word: But as truly as I live, all the earth shall be filled with the glory of the LORD. Because all those men which have seen my glory, and my miracles, which I did in Egypt and in the wilderness, and have tempted me now these ten times, and have not hearkened to my voice; Surely they shall not see the land which I sware unto their fathers, neither shall any of them that provoked me see it: But my servant Caleb, because he had another spirit with him, and hath followed me fully, him will I bring into the land whereinto he went; and his seed shall possess it*

When a land is under a siege the inheritance will be under bondage. A land can be a tribe, a community and a nation.
There are two major forces that keep a man under bondage in any given land or settlement.

A. Iniquity
Psalm 107 : 34- 39) *A fruitful land into barrenness, for the wickedness of*

them that dwell therein.Psalms:107:35: He turneth the wilderness into a standing water, and dry ground into watersprings.Psalms:107:36: And there he maketh the hungry to dwell, that they may prepare a city for habitation;Psalms:107:37: And sow the fields, and plant vineyards, which may yield fruits of increase.Psalms:107:38: He blesseth them also, so that they are multiplied greatly; and suffereth not their cattle to decrease.Psalms:107:39: Again, they are minished and brought low through oppression, affliction, and sorrow.

B. Satanic/demonic sacrifice

Num. 35:33-34 *So ye shall not pollute the land wherein ye are: for blood it defileth the land: and the land cannot be cleansed of the blood that is shed therein, but by the blood of him that shed it.*

Num.35:34 *Defile not therefore the land which ye shall inhabit, wherein I dwell: for I the LORD dwell among the children of Israel.#*

What happens, when the land is polluted?

A. The land is cursed and the people are stranded.

2 king 2:18-22 *And when they came again to him, (for he tarried at Jericho,) he said unto them, Did I not say unto you, Go not? And the men of the city said unto Elisha, Behold, I pray thee, the situation of this city is pleasant, as my lord seeth: but the water is naught, and the ground barren. And he said, Bring me a new cruse, and put salt therein. And they brought it to him. And he went forth unto the spring of the waters, and cast the salt in there, and said, Thus saith the LORD, I have healed these waters; there shall not be from thence any more death or barren land. So the waters were healed unto this day, according to the saying of Elisha which he spake.*

B. The giant and the forces of darkness hinder the people from taking their possession.

Num. 13:33 *And there we saw the giants, the sons of Anak, which come of the giants: and we were in our own sight as grasshoppers, and so we were in their sight.*

PRAYER POINTS ON:
DREAMS

1. Lord, by the blood of Jesus, I uproot every evil, done against me in the dream through witchcraft power in Jesus name.

2. Lord, any aspect of my life (marital, financial, career, fruitfulness, business promotion) that is under the control of witchcraft by your blood set me free today.

3. Today, I cut-off every controlling power of witchcraft over my life and family

4. Today, by the fire of the Holy Ghost, I proclaim death in the camp of all witches troubling my destiny.

PRAYER POINTS ON: FAMILIAR SPIRIT

1. Lord, every spirit of defilement that the enemy uses against my spirit, soul and body, I set them on fire today

2. Lord, all deliberate covenant I have entered into because of my ignorance, today I renounce all by the blood of Jesus.

3. Lord, any spirit husband or wife tormenting my body and marital life, I disconnect myself by the blood and I release God's judgement on them.

PRAYER POINTS ON: FAMILY MEMBERS.

1. Every arrow of sudden death calculated against me through a family member or relative, today, by the power of the blood of Jesus I return it back to the sender to kill them.

2. Lord, anywhere they are gathered to determine death sentence over my life and family, strike them to death by thunder.

3. Lord, any affliction I am going through, that household enemies are responsible for, I decree their mysterious death .

4. Lord, every household enemy responsible for my stagnation

in life bring them under speedy judgement and restore my lost glory.

PRAYER POINTS ON: FALSE PROPHET
1.	Lord destroy the habitation of false prophets, that are fighting against me, with an unquenchable fire.
2.	Lord, today, I send a strange wind from the throne of God to blow the camp and gathering of evil men into the sea of destruction.
3.	Lord, today bring me out of the cage of darkness, deliver me from the land of satanic oppression and restore my lost glory.
4.	Lord, every calamity ravaging my family through the invocation of witchcraft power and false prophet, today I return it back by fire to destroy them.

PRAYER POINTS ON: CULTURAL AFFLICTION
Prayer Points;
1.	Lord, every load of cultural affliction sitting over my destiny be removed by fire.
2.	Lord, anything that has been done on my behalf through sacrifice or incantations that's affecting my destiny, today I renounce it by the blood of Jesus.
3.	Lord, today by the fire of the Holy Ghost, remove the garment of shame, ridicule and stagnation from my life.
4.	By the blood of Jesus, every demonic deposit that has been released into my body and destiny through familiar spirit, I return it to the enemy to destroy them.

5.   Lord, in this month of the year, I take authority over the arrows of death, sickness, accident in my life, family and career.

6.   Lord, in 21 days, roast every witch and wizard troubling me and my family to death in Jesus name.

PRAYER POINTS ON: SPIRITUAL SHADOWS

1.   Lord, today by the intervention of the blood, deliver me from all enemies that rise up against me and I lay them to rest permanently.

2.   Lord, today by the blood of Jesus, I silence every voice of the enemy, through spiritual shadow, strange voices and manipulation.

3.   Lord, by the power of the Holy Spirit, I pull down every standing altar and power of the enemy calculated against my destined.

4.   Lord, as the year goes to an end, make my family and me to sing a new song.

5.   Lord, everyone that has said where is my God, give me a speedy miracle, that will decorate them with shame and divine judgement.

PRAYER POINT ON:
CIRCUMSTANCIAL NAME

1.   Lord lift me up above the battles of my life and make me too strong for my enemy to handle.

2.   Lord, today I reject every mark of affliction and oppression working against my divine health.

3.	Lord terminate every invisible mark of devourer, lack and want working against my finances and income.
4.	Lord every satanic power fighting against my career expose them.
5.	Lord every satanic garment covering my glory and hindering my favour remove it today.
6.	Lord, as the year goes to an end, decorate my family in a marvellous way. We shall not end this year in sorrow.

PRAYER POINTS ON: MANIPULLATION
1.	Today, by the blood of Jesus, I destroy the power and the wind of manipulation blowing against my destiny.
2.	All arrows of manipulation calculated against any aspect of my destiny, career, marriage, and finance, today I decree the fire of God to consume them.
3.	By the authority of God over my life, I command the wild wind from the throne of God to blow against all forms of manipulation monitoring my destiny.
4.	 By the blood of Jesus, I decree my total deliverance from every manipulation that moves a man against his destiny.

PRAYER POINTS ON: DEMONIC SACRIFICE
1.	Lord, I decree every land of my destiny to respond to fruitfulness, breakthroughs and success.
2.	Today, I curse in the name of the Lord, every force contending with my breakthrough in the land God has ordained for me.
3.	Lord by the power of the blood of Jesus, I decree every giant in my land be destroyed.

4.   Lord in this season of my life in this city I shall live and prosper above the forces of the land.

5.   Lord just like Isaac, enlarge my coast beyond the oppositions of the enemy.

CHAPTER EIGHT
WHEN GOD APPEARS, WHAT HAPPENS?

A. (GOD DELIVERS FROM FINANCIAL BONDAGE)

A Meaningful Life Depends Absolutely on the Grace and blessings of God. This is obtainable by right knowledge.

Fundamental Truth about Financial Blessing

1.   The blessing of redemption is not complete without living in riches.

2 **Cor.8.9** *For ye know the grace of our Lord Jesus Christ, that, though he was rich, yet for your sakes he became poor, that ye through his poverty might be rich.*

2.   Apart from the grace and help of God, your level of relevance, accomplishment and comfort in life, is determined by the level of the financial blessings you command.

Eccl.5:19 *Every man also to whom God hath given riches and wealth, and hath given him power to eat thereof, and to take his portion, and to rejoice in his labour; this is the gift of God.*

3.   God dignifies your life when your righteousness is decorated with financial blessings.

Ecc. 10:19 *A feast is made for laughter, and wine maketh merry: but money answereth all things.*

4.   The devil understands this strategy and decides to keep the people under bondage.

5.   Your earnest prayer this year, in the school of financial blessing should be 'Lord, this year, I don't want to be stressed; I only want to be helped; to be blessed'.

6. Jesus gave about 28 parables. 16 out of the 28 parables spoke about money.

7. Over 200 scriptures speak about money.

8. Any financial prosperity, either individual, corporalion or national that does not include God, has no future, because they can fail.

Gen. 47:15 *And when money failed in the land of Egypt, and in the land of Canaan, all the Egyptians came unto Joseph, and said, Give us bread: for why should we die in thy presence? for the money faileth.*

9. Understand that prosperity with spirituality is a possibility.

10. Understand that Jesus paid the price for you to prosper. (2Cor 8:9)

11. Understand that money has wings and God does not want you to labour in vain. (Prov. 23:5)

12. Understand that wealth without God, is building a future without a foundation.

Why do men go through financial stress?

1. **When the enemy is at work.**

(Eccl. 2:24) *There is nothing better for a man, than that he should eat and drink, and that he should make his soul enjoy good in his labour. This also I saw, that it was from the hand of God*

2. **When you break the covenant.**

Deut. 28:15 *But it shall come to pass, if thou wilt not hearken unto the voice of the LORD thy God, to observe to do all his commandments and his statutes which I command thee this day; that all these curses shall come upon thee, and overtake thee:*

3.	**When you lack investment:**
Eccl.7:25 *There is nothing better for a man, than that he should eat and drink, and that he should make his soul enjoy good in his labour. This also I saw, that it was from the hand of God.*
Eccl. 8:16 *When I applied mine heart to know wisdom, and to see the business that is done upon the earth: (for also there is that neither day nor night seeth sleep with his eyes:*
Prov.22:29. *Seest thou a man diligent in his business? he shall stand before kings; he shall not stand before mean men.*

"many people know why they are working, but not many know why they are living." (Beran wolf)

4.	**When you lack management of your excesses, planning, organisation and opportunities.**
Prov. 16:16) *How much better is it to get wisdom than gold! and to get understanding rather to be chosen than silver!*

5.	**When the forces of debt, borrowing, hire purchase, unguided spending take over your life.**

6.	**Wrong investment.**

7.	**When you are too confident without God, you create a crack in your destiny.**

8.	**When there is a curse upon the land or the seed of your business. Jos. 6:26.** *And Joshua adjured them at that time, saying, cursed be the man before the LORD, that riseth up and buildeth this city Jericho: he shall lay the foundation thereof in his firstborn, and in his youngests son shall he set up the gates of it.*

9.   No matter how financially disciplined you are, when a curse is at work,   your financial life can be grounded. Below are examples of financial devourers.

Case Study:1

A.   The pastor inherited two houses from the mother. After her death, he lodged the money from rent into the bank. After a while, he started having challenges in life. He waited on the Lord, God told him that it is blood money.

B.   Dreaming about seeing strange forces coming to cart away with your goods.
C.   Mysterious disappearance of your money physically.
D.   Re-occurrence of a given challenge when money appears. e.g. sickness.
E.   Anything you invest money into that doesn't yield results.
F.   Any project you do with your money which remains uncompleted.
G.   You packed into a house and everything is going down constantly.
H.   To be liberal with money, but find it difficult to secure financial help or favour is a curse.

Factors Responsible for Reckless Spending

A.   **Lack of contentment. (1 Timothy 6:6-11)** *but godliness with contentment is great gain. For we brought nothing into this world, and is certain we carry nothing out. And having food and raiment let us be therewith content. But they that will be rich fall into temptation and a snare, and into many foolish and hurtful lusts, which drown men in destruction and perdition. For the love of money is the root of all evil: which while some coveted after, they have erred from the faith, and pierced themselves through with many sorrows. But thou, O man of God, flee these things; and follow after righteousness,* *godliness, faith, love, patience, meekness.*

· Too many troubles around you that you don't have explanation for.

Eccl 4:1 *So I returned, and considered all the oppressions that are done under the sun: and behold the tears of such as were oppressed, and they had no comforter; and on the side of their oppressors there was power; but they had no comforter*

B. **Wrong investment. Eccl 10:15** *the labour of the foolish wearieth every one of them, because he knoweth not how to go to the city.*

The Strategies of the Enemy to Attack Your Finances.

(Ecc-2:24) *There is nothing better for a man, than that he should eat and drink, and that he should make his soul enjoy good in his labour. This also I saw, that it was from the hand of God.*

The enemy manifest in your finance through:

1. **Organized devourer. (Haggai 1:6)** *Ye have sown much, and bring in little; ye eat, but ye have not enough; ye drink, but ye are not filled with drink; ye clothe you, but there is none warm; and he that earneth wages earneth wages to put it into a bag with holes.*

2. **When the agent of the devil is at work:** e.g. The experience of someone collecting money from you in the dream; the devil moves you to steal what is not yours

Joshua 7:19 *And Joshua said unto Achan, My son, give, I pray thee, glory to the LORD God of Israel, and make confession unto him; and tell me now what thou hast done; hide it not from me.*

2 Kings 5:27 *the leprosy therefore of Naaman shall cleave unto thee, and unto thy seed for ever. And he went out from his presence a leper as white as snow.*

3. **When someone gives you money constantly with a left hand.**

4. **When someone requests from you the same amount of currency.**

5. **When someone buys something from you or employ**

you, but does not always pay you by himself.

6.	When someone gives you money on a particular day, week or hour of a month.

- **How to Handle the Devourer**
- 1.	**Ask God to grant you divine secrets to overcome any form of devourer around your finances.**
- 2.	**Renew your financial covenant with God.**

(Jer. 30:16) *Therefore all they that devour thee shall be devoured; and all thine adversaries, every one of them, shall go into captivity; and they that spoil thee shall be a spoil, and all that prey upon thee will I give for a prey.*

FINANCE AND INVESTMENT

According To Martin Luther King:

Any religion that claims to be concerned about people without addressing the economic conditions that strangle them is a dry and useless religion.

<u>WHY PEOPLE DO NOT HAVE INVESTMENT</u>

- Ø **Many workers spend more than what they earn**: For instance, statistics shows that in Britain, 80% of people owe more than they can pay, than they earn.
- Ø **Post retirement challenge:** At retirement in the United Kingdom, ninety percent of retirees cannot write their cheque, they do not have money. Nine out of ten people in Britain have to wait for the cheque every month.
- Ø **The effect of borrowing:** Sixty percent of the British population are borrowing above their own ability.
- Ø **The challenge of not utilising opportunities productively:** Financial freedom requires that you work smart and not work hard.

Ø **Effect of tax policies:** You pay tax four times in your life. When you earn, when you spend, when you save, and when you die.

Ø **When you desire pleasure before labour**: that is, desiring comfort before sacrifice in your career.

Prov. 24:27 *Prepare thy work without, and make it fit for thyself in the field; and afterwards build thine house.*

Prov. 27:24 *For riches are not for ever: and doth the crown endure to every generation?*

Deut. 28:8 *The LORD shall command the blessing upon thee in thy storehouses, and in all that thou settest thine hand unto; and he shall bless thee in the land which the LORD thy God giveth thee*

WHAT IS INVESTMENT?

Gen.26:1-4 *And there was a famine in the land, beside the first famine that was in the days of Abraham. And Isaac went unto Abimelech king of the Philistines unto Gerar. And the LORD appeared unto him, and said, Go not down into Egypt; dwell in the land which I shall tell thee of Sojourn in this land, and I will be with thee, and will bless thee; for unto thee, and unto thy seed, I will give all these countries, and I will perform the oath which I sware unto Abraham thy father; And I will make thy seed to multiply as the stars of heaven, and will give unto thy seed all these countries; and in thy seed shall all the nations of the earth be blessed;*

1. When you know and understand your season of sowing and reaping.
2. When you know when and where to plant.
3. When you secure an idea, instruction from the Lord, on what to do with your life and resources to live in financial freedom.
4. When you turn what you have into what you have not to get what you want.

WHEN GOD APPEARS, WHAT HAPPENS?

A.   **You Enjoy Family Rest .**

Text: job. 29:1-13 *Moreover Job continued his parable, and said, Oh that I were as in months past, as in the days when God preserved me;: When his candle shined upon my head, and when by his light I walked through darkness; As I was in the days of my youth, when the secret of God was upon my tabernacle; When the Almighty was yet with me, when my children were about me; When I washed my steps with butter, and the rock poured me out rivers of oil; When I went out to the gate through the city, when I prepared my seat in the street! The young men saw me, and hid themselves: and the aged arose, and stood up. The princes refrained talking, and laid their hand on their mouth. The nobles held their peace, and their tongue cleaved to the roof of their mouth. When the ear heard me, then it blessed me; and when the eye saw me, it gave witness to me: Because I delivered the poor that cried, and the fatherless, and him that had none to help him. The blessing of him that was ready to perish came upon me: and I caused the widow's heart to sing for joy.*

A Godly family is a home that enjoys the constant presence, helps, blessings and rest from God even in the midst of life challenges.

What does it mean to have a restful family?
1. To have God as the absolute owner of your family,
2. To have God fearing children.
3. To have God fearing parents.
4. To live a fulfilled life.
5. To enjoy generational blessings.

What is the value of having a restful family?

1.   You have children that fulfil their destiny.
2 Chronicles 6:7-10 *Now it was in the heart of David my father to build an house for the name of the LORD God of Israel.: But the LORD said to David my father, Forasmuch as it was in thine heart to build an house for my name, thou didst well in that it was in thine heart: Notwithstanding thou shalt not build the house; but thy son which shall come forth out of thy loins, he shall build the house for my name. The LORD therefore hath performed his word that he hath spoken: for I am risen up in the room of David my father, and am set on the throne of Israel, as the LORD promised, and have built the house for the name of the LORD God of Israel.*

2.   You have children that enjoy constant prophetic blessings.
Deut. 33:6-7 *Let Reuben live, and not die; and let not his men be few. And this is the blessing of Judah: and he said, Hear, LORD, the voice of Judah, and bring him unto his people: let his hands be sufficient for him; and be thou an help to him from his enemies.*

3.   You and your children will enjoy divine increase.
Ps. 115:9-14. *O Israel, trust thou in the LORD: he is their help and their shield. O house of Aaron, trust in the LORD: he is their help and their shield. Ye that fear the LORD, trust in the LORD: he is their help and their shield. The LORD hath been mindful of us: he will bless us; he will bless the house of Israel; he will bless the house of Aaron. He will bless them that fear the LORD, both small and great. The LORD shall increase you more and more, you and your children.*

4.   **You and your children will enjoy generational blessings.**

PS 78:1-8. *Give ear, O my people, to my law: incline your ears to the words of my mouth.Psalms:78:2: I will open my mouth in a parable: I will utter dark sayings of old: Which we have heard and known, and our fathers have told us. We will not hide them from their children, shewing to the generation to come the praises of the LORD, and his strength, and his wonderful works that he hath done. For he established a testimony in Jacob, and appointed a law in Israel, which he commanded our fathers, that they should make them known to their children: That the generation to come might know them, even the children which should be born; who should arise and declare them to their children: That they might set their hope in God, and not forget the works of God, but keep his commandments: And might not be as their fathers, a stubborn and rebellious generation; a generation that set not their heart aright, and whose spirit was not stedfast with God.*

5.   **You and your children will enjoy the mercy of God.**
Ps 103:17-18 *But the mercy of the LORD is from everlasting to everlasting upon them that fear him, and his righteousness unto children's children; To such as keep his covenant, and to those that remember his commandments to do them.*

6.   **You will flourish and bring forth fruits at old age.**
Ps. 92:12-14. *The righteous shall flourish like the palm tree: he shall grow like a cedar in Lebanon. Those that be planted in the house of the LORD shall flourish in the courts of our God. They shall still bring forth fruit in old age; they shall be fat and flourishing;*

7.   **God will make your seed (children) mighty and be a blessed generation.**
Ps. 112:1-2 *Praise ye the LORD. Blessed is the man that feareth the LORD, that delighteth greatly in his commandments. His seed shall be mighty upon earth: the generation of the upright shall be blessed.*

8.   **You will eat the fruits of the labour of thine hands.**

Ps. 128:2-6. *For thou shalt eat the labour of thine hands: happy shalt thou be, and it shall be well with thee. Thy wife shall be as a fruitful vine by the sides of thine house: thy children like olive plants round about thy table. Behold, that thus shall the man be blessed that feareth the LORD. The LORD shall bless thee out of Zion: and thou shalt see the good of Jerusalem all the days of thy life. Yea, thou shalt see thy children's children, and peace upon Israel.*

CHALLENGES OF UNRESTFUL HOME.

1.   **Rebellious children.**

Psalm 109:9,10 *Let his children be fatherless, and his wife a widow. Let his children be continually vagabonds, and beg: let them seek their bread also out of their desolate places.*

Psalm 144:11-15 *Rid me, and deliver me from the hand of strange children, whose mouth speaketh vanity, and their right hand is a right hand of falsehood: That our sons may be as plants grown up in their youth; that our daughters may be as corner stones, polished after the similitude of a palace: That our garners may be full, affording all manner of store: that our sheep may bring forth thousands and ten thousands in our streets: That our oxen may be strong to labour; that there be no breaking in, nor going out; that there be no complaining in our streets. Happy is that people, that is in such a case: yea, happy is that people, whose God is the LORD.*

2.   **Lack of Godly parents.**

(Jer. 35:1-6) ....And I set before the sons of the house of the Rechabites pots full of wine, and cups, and I said unto them, Drink ye wine. But they said, We will drink no wine: for Jonadab the son of Rechab our father commanded us, saying, Ye shall drink no wine, neither ye, nor your sons for ever:

Hear this relevant quote:

"Give me a generation of Christian women and I will undertake to change the whole of society within twelve months" **–Lord Shaftsbury.**

" Could I climb to the highest place in Athens, I would lift up my voice and proclaim, fellow citizens, why do you turn scrape every stone to gather wealth and take so little care of your children to whom one day you must relinquish all?".

–Lord Shaftsbury.

Hence, from the above quotes until Godly parenting becomes the order of the day in our society, rebellious children cannot be eradicated.

3.   **Ungodly pronouncement.**

(Gen.49:1-6) *And Jacob called unto his sons, and said, Gather yourselves together, that I may tell you that which shall befall you in the last days. Gather yourselves together, and hear, ye sons of Jacob; and hearken unto Israel your father. Reuben, thou art my firstborn, my might, and the beginning of my strength, the excellency of dignity, and the excellency of power: Unstable as water, thou shalt not excel; because thou wentest up to thy father's bed; then defiledst thou it: he went up to my couch. Simeon and Levi are brethren; instruments of cruelty are in their habitations. O my soul, come not thou into their secret; unto their assembly, mine honour, be not thou united: for in their anger they slew a man, and in their selfwill they digged down a wall.*

Every negative pronouncement, from the mouth of parents to their children is a seed of destruction into their destiny in the future. Until it is reversed such a child cannot escape a life of rebellion.

4.   **A spell. Num. 23:23** *God is not a man, that he should lie; neither the son of man, that he should repent: hath he said, and shall he not do it? or hath he spoken, and shall he not make it good?*

5.   **Bad company. 1Cor. 15:33** *Be not deceived: evil communications corrupt good manners.*

6.   **Initiation. Lev. 19:28** *Ye shall not make any cuttings in your flesh for the dead, nor print any marks upon you: I am the LORD.*

7.   **Godly parents, with ungodly lifestyle:** (In character, home management, domestic training and relationship with children).

Case study (A) the family of Isaac/Jacob

Gen. 25:20-27 *And Isaac was forty years old when he took Rebekah to wife, the daughter of Bethuel the Syrian of Padan-aram, the sister to Laban the Syrian. And Isaac intreated the LORD for his wife, because she was barren: and the LORD was intreated of him, and Rebekah his wife conceived. And the children struggled together within her; and she said, if it be so, why am I thus? And she went to enquire of the LORD. And the LORD said unto her, two nations are in thy womb, and two manner of people shall be separated from thy bowels; and the one people shall be stronger than the other people; and the elder shall serve the younger. And when her days to be delivered were fulfilled, behold, there were twins in her womb. And the first came out red, all over like an hairy garment; and they called his name Esau. And after that came his brother out, and his hand took hold on Esau's heel; and his name was called Jacob: and Isaac was threescore years old when she bare them. And the boys grew: and Esau was a cunning hunter, a man of the field; and Jacob was a plain man, dwelling in tents.*

Genesis 27:1-13 *And it came to pass, that when Isaac was old, and his eyes were dim, so that he could not see, he called Esau his eldest son, and said unto him, My son: and he said unto him, Behold, here am I. And he said, Behold now, I am old, I know not the day of my death: Now therefore take, I pray thee, thy weapons, thy quiver and thy bow, and go out to the field, and take me some venison; And make me savoury meat, such as I love, and bring it to me, that I may eat; that my soul may bless thee before I die. And Rebekah heard when Isaac spake to Esau his son. And Esau went to the field to hunt for venison, and to bring it. And Rebekah spake unto Jacob her son, saying, Behold, I heard thy father speak unto Esau thy brother, saying, Bring me venison, and make me savoury meat, that I may eat, and bless thee before the LORD before my death. Now therefore, my son, obey my voice according to that which I command thee. Go now to the flock, and fetch me from thence two good kids of the goats; and I will make them savoury meat for thy father, such as he loveth: And thou shalt bring it to thy father, that he may eat, and that he may bless thee before his death. And Jacob said to Rebekah his mother, Behold, Esau my brother is a hairy man, and I am a smooth man: My father peradventure will feel me, and I shall seem to him as* *a deceiver; and I shall bring a curse upon me, and not a blessing. And his mother said unto him, Upon me be thy curse, my son: only obey my voice, and go fetch me them. Alternate blessing twin to kill the brother, organized his escape*

Gen. 42-46 *And these words of Esau her elder son were told to Rebekah: and she sent and called Jacob her younger son, and said unto him, Behold, thy brother Esau, as touching thee, doth comfort himself, purposing to kill thee. Now therefore, my son, obey my voice; and arise, flee thou to Laban my brother to Haran; And tarry with him a few days, until thy brother's fury turn away; Until thy brother's anger turn away from thee, and he forget that which thou hast done to him: then I will send, and fetch thee from thence: why should I be deprived also of you both in one day? And Rebekah said to Isaac, I am weary of my life because of the daughters of Heth: if Jacob take a wife of the daughters of Heth, such as these which are of the daughters of the land, what good shall my life do me.*

Case study (B) the family of Nabal

1Sam. 25:1-25, *And Samuel died; and all the Israelites were gathered together, and lamented him, and buried him in his house at Ramah. And David arose, and went down to the wilderness of Paran. And there was a man in Maon, whose possessions were in Carmel; and the man was very great, and he had three thousand sheep, and a thousand goats: and he was shearing his sheep in Carmel. Now the name of the man was Nabal; and the name of his wife Abigail: and she was a woman of good understanding, and of a beautiful countenance: but the man was churlish and evil in his doings; and he was of the house of Caleb. And David heard in the wilderness that Nabal did shear his sheep. And David sent out ten young men, and David said unto the young men, Get you up to Carmel, and go to Nabal, and greet him in my name: And thus shall ye say to him that liveth in prosperity, Peace be both to thee, and peace be to thine house, and peace be unto all that thou hast. And now I have heard that thou hast shearers: now thy shepherds which were with us, we hurt them not, neither was there ought missing unto them, all the while they were in Carmel.*

1Sa:25:8: *Ask thy young men, and they will shew thee. Wherefore let the young men find favour in thine eyes: for we come in a good day: give, I pray thee,* *whatsoever cometh to thine hand unto thy servants, and to thy son David. And when David's young men came, they spake to Nabal according to all those words in the name of David, and ceased. And Nabal answered David's servants, and said, Who is David? and who is the son of Jesse? there be many servants now a days that break away every man from his master. Shall I then take my bread, and my water, and my flesh that I have killed for my shearers, and give it unto men, whom I know not whence they be? So David's young men turned their way, and went again, and came and told him all those sayings. And David said unto his men, Gird ye on every man his sword. And they girded on every man his sword; and David also girded on his sword: and there went up after David about four hundred men; and two hundred abode by the stuff. But one of the young men told Abigail, Nabal's wife, saying, Behold, David sent messengers out of the wilderness to salute our master; and he railed on them. But the men were very good unto us, and we were not hurt, neither missed we anything, as long as we were conversant with them, when we were in the fields: They were a wall unto us both by night and day, all the while we were with them keeping the sheep. Now therefore know and consider what thou wilt do; for evil is determined against our master, and against all his household: for he is such a son of Belial, that a man cannot speak to him. Then Abigail made haste, and took two hundred loaves, and two bottles of wine, and five sheep ready dressed, and five measures of parched corn, and an hundred clusters of raisins, and two hundred cakes of figs, and laid them on asses. And she said unto her servants, Go on before me; behold, I come after you. But she told not her husband Nabal. And it was so, as she rode on the ass, that she came down by the covert of the hill, and, behold, David and his men came down against her; and she met them. Now David had said, Surely in vain have I kept all that this fellow hath in the wilderness, so that nothing was missed of all that pertained unto him: and he hath requited me evil for good. So and more also do God unto the enemies of David, if I leave of all that pertain to him by the morning light any that pisseth against the wall. And when Abigail saw David, she hasted, and lighted off the ass, and fell before David on her face, and bowed herself to the ground, And fell at his feet, and said, Upon me, my lord, upon me let this iniquity be: and let thine handmaid, I pray thee, speak in thine audience, and hear the words of thine handmaid. Let not my lord, I pray thee, regard this man of Belial, even Nabal: for as his name is, so is he; Nabal is his name, and folly is with him: but I thine handmaid saw not the young men of my lord, whom thou didst send.*

8. Conspiracy for blessings.
Case Study (C) Jacob

Gen. 27:1-13 *And it came to pass, that when Isaac was old, and his eyes were dim, so that he could not see, he called Esau his eldest son, and said unto him, My son: and he said unto him, Behold, here am I. Ge:27:2: And he said, Behold now, I am old, I know not the day of my death: Now therefore take, I pray thee, thy weapons, thy quiver and thy bow, and go out to the field, and take me some venison; And make me savoury meat, such as I love, and bring it to me, that I may eat; that my soul may bless thee before I die. And Rebekah heard when Isaac spake to Esau his son. And Esau went to the field to hunt for venison, and to bring it. And Rebekah spake unto Jacob her son, saying, Behold, I heard thy father speak unto Esau thy brother, saying, Bring me venison, and make me savoury meat, that I may eat, and bless thee before the LORD before my death. Now therefore, my son, obey my voice according to that which I command thee. Go now to the flock, and fetch me from thence two good kids of the goats; and I will make them savoury meat for thy father, such as he loveth: And thou shalt bring it to thy father, that he may eat, and that he may bless thee before his death. And Jacob said to Rebekah his mother, Behold, Esau my brother is a hairy man, and I am a smooth man: My father peradventure will feel me, and I shall seem to him as a deceiver; and I shall bring a curse upon me, and not a blessing. And his mother said unto him, Upon me be thy curse, my son: only obey my voice, and go fetch me them.*

9. Alternative blessings.

Case Study (D) of Jacob

Gen 27:38-41 *And Esau said unto his father, Hast thou but one blessing, my father? bless me, even me also, O my father. And Esau lifted up his voice, and wept. And Isaac his father answered and said unto him, Behold, thy dwelling shall be the fatness of the earth, and of the dew of heaven from above;: And by thy sword shalt thou live, and shalt serve thy brother; and it shall come to pass when thou shalt have the dominion, that thou shalt break his yoke from off thy neck. And Esau hated Jacob because of the blessing wherewith his father blessed him: and Esau said in his heart, The days of mourning for my father are at hand; then will I slay my brother Jacob.*

10. **Parental Conspiracy.**
Case Study (E) of Jacob

Gen. 27:42-46 *And these words of Esau her elder son were told to Rebekah: and she sent and called Jacob her younger son, and said unto him, Behold, thy brother Esau, as touching thee, doth comfort himself, purposing to kill thee. Now therefore, my son, obey my voice; and arise, flee thou to Laban my brother to Haran; And tarry with him a few days, until thy brother's fury turn away; Until thy brother's anger turn away from thee, and he forget that which thou hast done to him: then I will send, and fetch thee from thence: why should I be deprived also of you both in one day? And Rebekah said to Isaac, I am weary of my life because of the daughters of Heth: if Jacob take a wife of the daughters of Heth, such as these which are of the daughters of the land, what good shall my life do me?*

11. **Lack of Godly wisdom in family management.**
Case Study (F) of Nabal

1Sam.25:1-25 *And Samuel died; and all the Israelites were gathered together, and lamented him, and buried him in his house at Ramah. And David arose, and went down to the wilderness of Paran. And there was a man in Maon, whose possessions were in Carmel; and the man was very great, and he had three thousand sheep, and a thousand goats: and he was shearing his sheep in Carmel. Now the name of the man was Nabal; and the name of his wife Abigail: and she was a woman of good understanding, and of a beautiful countenance: but the man was churlish and evil in his doings; and he was of the house of Caleb. And David heard in the wilderness that Nabal did shear his sheep. And David sent out ten young men, and David said unto the young men, Get you up to Carmel, and go to Nabal, and greet him in my name: And thus shall ye say to him that liveth in prosperity, Peace be both to thee, and peace be to thine house, and peace be unto all that thou hast. And now I have heard that thou hast shearers: now thy shepherds which were with us, we hurt them not, neither was there ought missing unto them, all the while they were in Carmel. Ask thy young men, and they will shew thee. Wherefore let the young men find favour in thine eyes: for we come in a good day: give, I pray thee, whatsoever cometh to thine hand unto thy servants, and to thy son David. And when David's young men came, they spake to Nabal according to all those words in the name of David, and ceased. And Nabal answered David's servants, and said, Who is David? and who is the son of Jesse? there be many servants now a days that break away every man from his master. Shall I then take my bread, and my water, and my flesh that I have killed for my shearers, and give it unto men, whom I know not whence they be? So David's young men turned their way, and went again, and came and told him all those sayings. And David said unto his men, Gird ye on every man his sword. And they girded on every man his sword; and David also girded on his sword: and there went up after David about four hundred men; and two hundred abode by the stuff. But one of the young men told Abigail, Nabal's wife, saying, Behold, David sent messengers out of the wilderness to salute our master; and he railed on them. But the men were very good unto us, and we were not hurt, neither missed we anything, as long as we were conversant with them, when we were in the fields: They were a wall unto us both by night and day, all the while we were with them keeping the sheep. Now therefore know and consider what thou wilt do; for evil is determined against our master, and against all his household: for he is such a son of Belial, that a man cannot speak to him. Then Abigail made haste, and took two hundred loaves, and two bottles of wine, and five sheep ready dressed, and five measures of parched corn, and an hundred clusters of raisins, and two hundred cakes of figs, and laid them on asses. And she said unto her servants, Go on before me; behold, I come after you. But she told not her husband Nabal. And it was so, as she rode on the ass, that she came down by the covert of the hill, and, behold, David and his men came down against her; and she met them. Now David had said, surely in vain have I kept all that this fellow hath in the wilderness, so that nothing was missed of all that pertained unto him: and he hath requited me evil for good. So and more also do God unto the enemies of David, if I leave of all that pertain to him by the morning light any that pisseth against the wall. And when Abigail saw David, she hasted, and lighted off the ass, and fell before David on her face, and bowed herself to the ground, And fell at his feet, and said, Upon me, my lord, upon me let this iniquity be: and let thine handmaid, I pray thee, speak in thine audience, and hear the words of thine handmaid. Let not my lord, I pray thee, regard this man of Belial, even Nabal: for as his name is, so is he; Nabal is his name, and folly is with him: but I thine handmaid saw not the young men of my lord, whom thou didst send.*

How do I overcome the challenges of unrestful family?

1.   **Raise an altar of prayers constantly for your children.**
(**Is.65:23.**) *They shall not labour in vain, nor bring forth for trouble; for they are the seed of the blessed of the LORD, and their offspring with them.*

2.   **Ask the Lord to take over the heart of your children and teach them His ways.**
Is. 54:13 *And all thy children shall be taught of the LORD; and great shall be the peace of thy children.*

3.   **Ask God to deliver you from the forces of life that turn the heart of children against God and their parents.**
Ps. 144:11-15 *Rid me, and deliver me from the hand of strange children, whose mouth speaketh vanity, and their right hand is a right hand of falsehood: That our sons may be as plants grown up in their youth; that our daughters may be as corner stones, polished after the similitude of a palace: That our garners may be full, affording all manner of store: that our sheep may bring forth thousands and ten thousands in our streets:*

That our oxen may be strong to labour; that there be no breaking in, nor going out; that there be no complaining in our streets. Happy is that people, that is in such a case: yea, happy is that people, whose God is the LORD.

4.   Enforce the principles of God into your family.

Prov. 22:6 *Train up a child in the way he should go: and when he is old, he will not depart from it.*

5.   Ask for the help of God to live with your spouse in the wisdom of God.

1 Peter 3:7 *Likewise, ye husbands, dwell with them according to knowledge, giving honour unto the wife, as unto the weaker vessel, and as being heirs together of the grace of life; that your prayers be not hindered.*

Prov. 14:1 *Every wise woman buildeth her house: but the foolish plucketh it down with her hands.*

PRAYER POINTS ON:
FINANCE AND INVESTMENT

1.   Lord, deliver me today from every force of life that makes a man to labour without result.

2.   Lord from every spirit of poverty that has plagued my family not to be a partaker of prosperity set me free today.

3.   Lord, from every load of the devil sitting over my finance, today set me free.

4.   Lord, from every force of life that will not allow my hands to handle and retain money, today set me free.

5.   Lord, from every wind of devourer that consumes my financial blessings and keep me under the yoke of lack and want, today set me free.

6.   Lord, deliver me from the spirit of financial slavery that comes through borrowing, begging, wasteful spending and afflictions, in Jesus name.

7.   Lord, expose every evil around my life responsible for my financial calamity, in Jesus name.

8.   Lord break the yoke of poverty over my life and the works of

my hand.

9.	Lord open my eyes to know what to do to prosper.

10.	Lord deliver me from financial wilderness.

11.	Lord grant me financial rest this year, My hands shall not lack money, my mouth shall not lack water and bread, my business and career shall not lack favour.

12.	Lord in my family make me a financial voice for generational blessing and not a devourer.

13.	Every door of financial blessing, that has been shut against me, I command it to be open.

14.	Lord, by your blood, today I destroy the root of financial curse in my life.

15.	Lord, by your blood, deliver me from every form of financial bondage.

16.	Lord, turn my financial stress to financial rest.

17.	Lord, every force of darkness that hinders my financial favour, be terminated on this mountain.

18.	Lord, from every satanic force that moves a man to waste his financial resources, by your blood deliver me today.

19.	Lord, in a miraculous way enlarge my coast and make me a blessing among my equals.

20.	Lord, open my eyes to the secrets of Abraham and Isaac that will deliver me from poverty forever.

21.	Lord, today by the blood of Jesus, I decree everlasting judgement against the forces of poverty.

22.	Lord, by your blood today deliver me from the forces that move men to be a victim of wrong investment and losses.

23.	Lord, by your blood today heal my root and destiny of financial curse.

24.	Lord, by your blessings make me a man that can take care of himself, family and future.

25.	Lord, from every form of incapacity in my life (spiritual, physical) that will not allow me to enjoy financial prosperity, today set me free.

26.   Lord, let every cloud of darkness hanging over my life and the work of my hands today be terminated.

27.   Lord I decree the door of financial favour to open for me that will change my story forever.

28.   Lord, make me a pillar in your kingdom.

29.   Lord this year, concerning the works of my hands, turn my sweat to rest.

PRAYER POINTS ON:
FAMILY REST

1.   Lord, all the children you have given me, I return them to you, take over their spirit, soul and body for your glory.

2.   Lord, all the children you have given to me, make them a generational blessing and grant me rest.

3.   Lord, tonight by the blood of Jesus, I destroy the strong hold of the enemy over the destiny of my children.

4.   Lord, I shall not bring forth for trouble, none of my children shall bring me shame.

5.   Lord every force of devourer that destroy the destiny of children shall not gain access into my children and family.

6.   Lord my age shall be years of rest, flourishing and sound health.

7.   Lord I will not use my hand to destroy my home.

8.   Lord my children shall not turn against me.

9.   Lord, I shall live long to eat the fruit of my labour.

10.   Lord, make my family your dwelling place.

11.   Lord, open my eyes to see what I don't know about my home and children.

12.   Lord, make my family your dwelling place.

WHEN GOD APPEARS WHAT HAPPENS?
A. DIVINE JUDGEMENT

v   Life battles are real

v   Man is ordained by covenant to win all battles.

v   Man is not empowered to fight all battles. There are battles only God can see, fight and conquer. But the victory goes to man and the glory goes to God.

v   God determines which battle you win.

v   God takes over our battles through various instrument of judgement.

v   God's divine judgement is ordained to silence all your enemies forever.

WHAT IS DIVINE JUDGEMENT?

v   It means God executing total destruction in the camp of the enemy.

Jer. 50:25 *The LORD hath opened his armoury, and hath brought forth the weapons of his indignation: for this is the work of the Lord GOD of hosts in the land of the Chaldeans.,*

Jer.33:34. *Considerest thou not what this people have spoken, saying, The two families which the LORD hath chosen, he hath even cast them off? thus they have despised my people, that they should be no more a nation before*

v   It means God taking vengeance upon the enemy in favour of the saints.

(Isaiah49:24-26 *Shall the prey be taken from the mighty, or the lawful captive delivered? But thus saith the LORD, Even the captives of the mighty shall be taken away, and the prey of the terrible shall be delivered: for I will contend with him that contendeth with thee, and I will save thy children. And I will feed them that oppress thee with their own flesh; and they shall be drunken with their own blood, as with sweet wine: and all flesh shall know that I the LORD am thy Saviour and thy Redeemer, the mighty One of Jacob.*

v   It is God empowering us above our enemies to subdue them. **Jer. 51:20-23** *Thou art my battle axe and weapons of war: for with thee will I break in pieces the nations, and with thee will I destroy kingdoms; And with thee will I break in pieces the horse and his rider; and with thee will I break in pieces the chariot and his rider; With thee also will I break in pieces man and woman; and with thee will I break in pieces old and young; and with thee will I break in pieces the young man and the maid;*

Who is God in the school of divine judgement?
1.   **God is an Afflicter. 2Kings. 17:20** *Behold, the days come, that all that is in thine house, and that which thy fathers have laid up in store unto this day, shall be carried into Babylon: nothing shall be left, saith the LORD.*
2.   **God is a Killer. 1 Samuel. 2:6** *The LORD killeth, and maketh alive: he bringeth down to the grave, and bringeth up.*

INSTRUMENTS OF GOD'S JUDGEMENT
1.   **Direct heavenly battles. Joshua 10:11-14** *And it came to pass, as they fled from before Israel, and were in the going down to Beth-horon, that the LORD cast down great stones from heaven upon them unto Azekah, and they died: they were more which died with hailstones than they whom the children of Israel slew with the sword. Then spake Joshua to the LORD in the day when the LORD delivered up the Amorites before the children of Israel, and he said in the sight of Israel, Sun, stand thou still upon Gibeon; and thou, Moon, in the valley of Ajalon.Jos:10:13: And the sun stood still, and the moon stayed, until the people had avenged themselves upon their enemies. Is not this written in the book of Jasher? So the sun stood still in the midst of heaven, and hasted not to go down about a whole day. And there was no day like that before it or after it, that the LORD hearkened unto the voice of a man: for the LORD fought for Israel.*

2.   **Angelic intervention: Isaiah 37:33-36** *Therefore thus saith the LORD concerning the king of Assyria, He shall not come into this city, nor shoot an arrow there nor come before it with shields, nor cast a bank against it. By the way that he came, by the same shall he return, and shall not come into this city, saith the LORD. For I will defend this city to save it for mine own sake, and for my servant David's sake. Then the angel of the LORD went forth, and smote in the camp of the Assyrians a hundred and fourscore and five thousand: and when they arose early in the morning, behold, they were all dead corpses.,*
2kings. 19:35, *And it came to pass that night, that the angel of the LORD went out, and smote in the camp of the Assyrians an hundred fourscore and five thousand: and when they arose early in the morning, behold, they were all dead corpses.*
Ps.34:7 *The angel of the LORD encampeth round about them that fear him, and delivereth them.*

3.   **The carpenters. Zech. 1:18-21** *Then lifted I up mine eyes, and saw, and behold four horns. And I said unto the angel that talked with me, What be these? And he answered me, These are the horns which have scattered Judah, Israel, and Jerusalem. And the LORD shewed me four carpenters.: Then said I, What come these to do? And he spake, saying, which lifted up their horn over the land of Judah to scatter it.*

4.   **The fishers and hunters. Jer.16:16** *Behold, I will send for many fishers, saith the LORD, and they shall fish them; and after will I send for many hunters, and they shall hunt them from every mountain, and from every hill, and out of the holes of the rocks.*

5.   **The earth. Jer. 22:29** *O earth, earth, earth, hear the word of the LORD*

Gen.4:9-12 *And the LORD said unto Cain, Where is Abel thy brother? And he said, I know not: Am I my brother's keeper? And he said, What hast thou done? the voice of thy brother's blood crieth unto me from the ground. And now art thou cursed from the earth, which hath opened her mouth to receive thy brother's blood from thy hand; When thou tillest the ground, it shall not* *henceforth yield unto thee her strength; a fugitive and a vagabond shalt thou be in the earth.*

6.   **The spirit of judgement.** (prophesy against something or someone) **Ezekiel. 11:4- 13** *Therefore prophesy against them, prophesy, O son of man. And the Spirit of the LORD fell upon me, and said unto me, Speak; Thus saith the LORD; Thus have ye said, O house of Israel: for I know the things that come into your mind, every one of them. Ye have multiplied your slain in this city, and ye have filled the streets thereof with the slain. Therefore thus saith the Lord GOD; Your slain whom ye have laid in the midst of it, they are the flesh, and this city is the caldron: but I will bring you forth out of the midst of it. Ye have feared the sword; and I will bring a sword upon you, saith the Lord GOD. And I will bring you out of the midst thereof, and deliver you into the hands of strangers, and will execute judgments among you. Ye shall fall by the sword; I will judge you in the border of Israel; and ye shall know that I am the LORD. This city shall not be your caldron, neither shall ye be the flesh in the midst thereof; but I will judge you in the border of Israel: And ye shall know that I am the LORD: for ye have not walked in my statutes, neither executed my judgments, but have done after the manners of the heathen that are round about you. And it came to pass, when I prophesied, that Pelatiah the son of Benaiah died. Then fell I down upon my face, and cried with a loud voice, and said, Ah Lord GOD! wilt thou make a full end of the remnant of Israel?*, Ezekiel 28:20-23. *Again the word of the LORD came unto me, saying, Son of man, set thy face against Zidon, and prophesy against it, And say, Thus saith the Lord GOD; Behold, I am against thee, O Zidon; and I will be glorified in the midst of thee: and they shall know that I am the LORD, when I shall have executed judgments in her, and shall be sanctified in her. For I will send into her pestilence, and blood into her streets; and the wounded shall be judged in the midst of her by the sword upon her on every side; and they shall know that I am the LORD.*

7.   **The wind. Ezekiel 37:9-14** *Then said he unto me, Prophesy untothe wind, prophesy, son of man, and say to the wind, Thus saith the Lord*

GOD; Come from the four winds, O breath, and breathe upon these slain, that they may   live. So I prophesied as he commanded me, and the breath came into them, and they lived, and stood up upon their feet, an exceeding great army. Then he said unto me, Son of man, these bones are the whole house of Israel: behold, they say, Our bones are dried, and our hope is lost: we are cut off for our parts. Therefore prophesy and say unto them, Thus saith the Lord GOD; Behold, O my people, I will open your graves, and cause you to come up out of your graves, and bring you into the land of Israel.: And ye shall know that I am the LORD, when I have opened your graves, O my people, and brought you up out of your graves, And shall put my spirit in you, and ye shall live, and I shall place you in your own land: then shall ye know that I the LORD have spoken it, and performed it, saith the LORD.

8.   **Prophetic mantle. 1 Sam. 15:25-28**, *now therefore, I pray thee, pardon my sin, and turn again with me, that I may worship the LORD. And Samuel said unto Saul, I will not return with thee: for thou hast rejected the word of the LORD, and the LORD hath rejected thee from being king over Israel. And as Samuel turned about to go away, he laid hold upon the skirt of his mantle, and it rent. And Samuel said unto him, The LORD hath rent the kingdom of Israel from thee this day, and hath given it to a neighbour of thine, that is better than thou.*

9.   **The spirit of just men made perfect:** Invoking the spirit of men, both dead and alive for divine judgement. *(Elijah and Elisha).* **2 Kings 2:1-14,** *And it came to pass, when the LORD would take up Elijah into heaven by a whirlwind, that Elijah went with Elisha from Gilgal. And Elijah said unto Elisha, Tarry here, I pray thee; for the LORD hath sent me to Bethel. And Elisha said unto him, As the LORD liveth, and as thy soul liveth, I will not leave thee. So they went down to Bethel. And the sons of the prophets that were at Bethel came forth to Elisha, and said unto him, Knowest thou that the LORD will take away thy master from thy head to day? And he said, Yea, I know it; hold ye your peace. And Elijah said unto him, Elisha, tarry here, I pray thee; for the LORD hath sent me to Jericho.*

And he said, As the LORD liveth, and as thy soul liveth, I will not leave thee. So they came to Jericho.

Judge. 7:17-20, *And he said unto them, Look on me, and do likewise: and, behold, when I come to the outside of the camp, it shall be that, as I do, so shall ye do. When I blow with a trumpet, I and all that are with me, then blow ye the trumpets also on every side of all the camp, and say, The sword of the LORD, and of Gideon. So Gideon, and the hundred men that were with him, came unto the outside of the camp in the beginning of the middle watch; and they had but newly set the watch: and they blew the trumpets, and brake the pitchers that were in their hands.: And the three companies blew the trumpets, and brake the pitchers, and held the lamps in their left hands, and the trumpets in their right hands to blow withal: and they cried, The sword of the LORD, and of Gideon.*

1 Sam. 28:6-18, *And when Saul enquired of the LORD, the LORD answered him not, neither by dreams nor by Urim, nor by prophets. Then said Saul unto his servants, Seek me a woman that hath a familiar spirit, that I may go to her, and enquire of her. And his servants said to him, Behold, there is a woman that hath a familiar spirit at Endor: And Saul disguised himself, and put on other raiment, and he went, and two men with him, and they came to the woman by night: and he said, I pray thee, divine unto me by the familiar spirit, and bring me him up, whom I shall name unto thee. And the woman said unto him, Behold, thou knowest what Saul hath done, how he hath cut off those that have familiar spirits, and the wizards, out of the land: wherefore then layest thou a snare for my life, to cause me to die? And Saul sware to her by the LORD, saying, As the LORD liveth, there shall no punishment happen to thee for this thing. Then said the woman, Whom shall I bring up unto thee? And he said, Bring me up Samuel. And when the woman saw Samuel, she cried with a loud voice: and the woman spake to Saul, saying, Why hast thou deceived me? For thou art Saul. And the king said unto her, Be not afraid: for what sawest thou? And the woman said unto Saul, I saw gods ascending out of the earth. And he said unto her, What form is he of? And she said, an old man cometh up; and he* *is covered with a mantle. And Saul perceived that it was Samuel, and he stooped with his face to the ground, and bowed himself. And Samuel said to Saul, Why hast thou disquieted me, to bring me up? And Saul answered, I am sore distressed; for the Philistines make war against me, and God is departed from me, and answereth me no more, neither by prophets, nor by dreams: therefore I have called thee, that thou mayest make known unto me what I shall do. Then said Samuel, Wherefore then dost thou ask of me, seeing the LORD is departed from thee, and is become thine enemy?: And the LORD hath done to him, as he spake by me: for the LORD hath rent the kingdom out of thine hand, and given it to thy neighbour, even to David: Because thou obeyedst not the voice of the LORD, nor executedst his fierce wrath upon Amalek, therefore hath the LORD done this thing unto thee this day*

Mark. 9:2-5 *And after six days Jesus taketh with him Peter, and James, and John, and leadeth them up into an high mountain apart by themselves: and he was transfigured before them. And his raiment became shining, exceeding white as snow; so as no fuller on earth can white them. And there appeared unto them Elias with Moses: and they were talking with Jesus. And Peter answered and said to Jesus, Master, it is good for us to be here: and let us make three tabernacles; one for thee, and one for Moses, and one for Elias. Evil spirit.*

10.   **Evil spirit. 1Kings. 22:20-23** *And the LORD said, Who shall persuade Ahab, that he may go up and fall at Ramoth-gilead? And one said on this manner, and another said on that manner. And there came forth a spirit, and stood before the LORD, and said, I will persuade him. And the LORD said unto him, Wherewith? And he said, I will go forth, and I will be a lying spirit in the mouth of all his prophets. And he said, Thou shalt persuade him, and prevail also: go forth, and do so. Now therefore, behold, the LORD hath put a lying spirit in the mouth of all these thy prophets, and the LORD hath spoken evil concerning thee.*

Judges 9:1-23 *And Abimelech the son of Jerubbaal went to Shechem unto his mother's brethren, and communed with them, and with all the family of the house* *of his mother's father, saying, Speak, I pray you, in the ears of all the men of Shechem, Whether is better for you, either that all the sons of Jerubbaal, which are threescore and ten persons, reign over you, or that one reign over you? remember also that I am your bone and your flesh. And his mother's brethren spake of him in the ears of all the men of Shechem all these words: and their hearts inclined to follow Abimelech; for they said, He is our brother.4: And they gave him threescore and ten pieces of silver out of the house of Baal-berith, wherewith Abimelech hired vain and light persons, which followed him. And he went unto his father's house at Ophrah, and slew his brethren the sons of Jerubbaal, being threescore and ten persons, upon one stone: notwithstanding yet Jotham the youngest son of Jerubbaal was left; for he hid himself:6: And all the men of Shechem gathered together, and all the house of Millo, and went, and made Abimelech king, by the plain of the pillar that was in Shechem: And when they told it to Jotham, he went and stood in the top of mount Gerizim, and lifted up his voice, and cried, and said unto them, Hearken unto me, ye men of Shechem, that God may hearken unto you. The trees went forth on a time to anoint a king over them; and they said unto the olive tree, Reign thou over us. But the olive tree said unto them, Should I leave my fatness, wherewith by me they honour God and man, and go to be promoted over the trees?: And the trees said to the fig tree, Come thou, and reign over us.: But the fig tree said unto them, Should I forsake my sweetness, and my good fruit, and go to be promoted over the trees? Then said the trees unto the vine, Come thou, and reign over us.: And the vine said unto them, Should I leave my wine, which cheereth God and man, and go to be promoted over the trees?: Then said all the trees unto the bramble, Come thou, and reign over us. And the bramble said unto the trees, If in truth ye anoint me king over you, then come and put your trust in my shadow: and if not, let fire come out of the bramble, and devour the cedars of Lebanon. Now therefore, if ye have done truly and sincerely, in that ye have made Abimelech king, and if ye have dealt well with Jerubbaal and his house, and have done unto him according to the deserving of his hands; (For my father fought for you, and adventured his life far, and delivered you out of the hand of Midian: And ye are risen up against my father's house this day, and have slain his sons, threescore and ten persons, upon*

113

one stone, and have made Abimelech, the son of his maidservant, king over the men of Shechem, because he is your brother;) If ye then have dealt truly and sincerely with Jerubbaal and with his house this day, then rejoice ye in Abimelech, and let him also rejoice in you: But if not, let fire come out from Abimelech, and devour the men of Shechem, and the house of Millo; and let fire come out from the men of Shechem, and from the house of Millo, and devour Abimelech. And Jotham ran away, and fled, and went to Beer, and dwelt there, for fear of Abimelech his brother. When Abimelech had reigned three years over Israel,9:23: Then God sent an evil spirit between Abimelech and the men of Shechem; and the men of Shechem dealt treacherously with Abimelech:

11.   **Arrow/bow. 2 Kings 13:15-19** *And Elisha said unto him, Take bow and arrows. And he took unto him bow and arrows. 13:16: And he said to the king of Israel, Put thine hand upon the bow. And he put his hand upon it: and Elisha put his hands upon the king's hands. And he said, Open the window eastward. And he opened it. Then Elisha said, Shoot. And he shot. And he said, The arrow of the LORD's deliverance, and the arrow of deliverance from Syria: for thou shalt smite the Syrians in Aphek, till thou have consumed them. And he said, Take the arrows. And he took them. And he said unto the king of Israel, Smite upon the ground. And he smote thrice, and stayed. And the man of God was wroth with him, and said, Thou shouldest have smitten five or six times; then hadst thou smitten Syria till thou hadst consumed it: whereas now thou shalt smite Syria but thrice. (prophetic symbol)*

12.   **A blast. 2 Kings 19:5-7** *So the servants of king Hezekiah came to Isaiah. And Isaiah said unto them, Thus shall ye say to your master, Thus saith the LORD, Be not afraid of the words which thou hast heard, with which the servants of the king of Assyria have blasphemed me. Behold, I will send a blast upon him, and he shall hear a rumour, and shall return to his own land; and I will cause him to fall by the sword in his own land.*

13.   **Your mouth is a weapon of warfare designed by God to silence your enemies.   Jer. 4:10-12** *Then said I, Ah, Lord GOD! Surely thou hast greatly deceived this people and Jerusalem, saying, ye shall have peace; whereas the sword reacheth unto the soul. At that time shall it be said to this people and to Jerusalem, A dry wind of the high places in the wilderness toward the daughter of my people, not to fan, nor to cleanse, Even a full wind from those places shall come unto me: now also will I give sentence against them.* **Ps. 120:7** *I am for peace: but when I speak, they are for war.*

WHY DO YOU NEED DIVINE JUDGEMENT?

1.   **To Secure Your Destiny.   Genesis 4:9-26** *And the LORD said unto Cain, Where is Abel thy brother? And he said, I know not: Am I my brother's keeper? And he said, What hast thou done? the voice of thy brother's blood crieth unto me from the ground. And now art thou cursed from the earth, which hath opened her mouth to receive thy brother's blood from thy hand; When thou tillest the ground, it shall not henceforth yield unto thee her strength; a fugitive and a vagabond shalt thou be in the earth. And Cain said unto the LORD, My punishment is greater than I can bear.: Behold, thou hast driven me out this day from the face of the earth; and from thy face shall I be hid; and I shall be a fugitive and a vagabond in the earth; and it shall come to pass, that everyone that findeth me shall slay me. And the LORD said unto him, Therefore whosoever slayeth Cain, vengeance shall be taken on him sevenfold. And the LORD set a mark upon Cain, lest any finding him should kill him. And Cain went out from the presence of the LORD, and dwelt in the land of Nod, on the east of Eden. And Cain knew his wife; and she conceived, and bare Enoch: and he builded a city, and called the name of the city, after the name of his son, Enoch. And unto Enoch was born Irad: and Irad begat Mehujael: and Mehujael begat Methusael: and Methusael begat Lamech. And Lamech took unto him two wives: the name of the one was Adah, and the name of the other Zillah. And Adah bare Jabal: he was the father of such as dwell in tents, and of such as have cattle. And his brother's name was Jubal: he was the father of all such as handle the harp and organ. And Zillah, she also bare Tubal-cain, an instructer of every artificer in*

115

brass and iron: and the sister of Tubal-cain was Naamah. And Lamech said unto his wives, Adah and Zillah, Hear my voice; ye wives of Lamech, hearken unto my speech: for I have slain a man to my wounding, and a young man to my hurt. If Cain shall be avenged sevenfold, truly Lamech seventy and sevenfold. And Adam knew his wife again; and she bare a son, and called his name Seth: For God, said she, hath appointed me another seed instead of Abel, whom Cain slew. And to Seth, to him also there was born a son; and he called his name Enos: then began men to call upon the name of the LORD.

2.	**To Cut Off The Hand Of The Enemy Over Your Life. Micah. 5:9,12** *Thine hand shall be lifted up upon thine adversaries, and all thine enemies shall be cut off. And I will cut off witchcrafts out of thine hand; and thou shalt have no more soothsayers:*

3.	**To restore all that the enemy has stolen. Prov. 6:31** *But if he be found, he shall restore sevenfold; he shall give all the substance of his house.*

4.	**To undo all the hand writing of the enemy over your life. Col. 2:14** *Blotting out the handwriting of ordinances that was against us, which was contrary to us, and took it out of the way, nailing it to his cross;*

5.	**To secure the mark of divine preservation. Heb. 11:28** *Through faith he kept the passover, and the sprinkling of blood, lest he that destroyed the firstborn should touch them.*

THE MINISTRY OF ANGELS

1.	**Angels are instruments of warfare: Rev:15:1-8** *And I saw another sign in heaven, great and marvellous, seven angels having the seven last plagues; for in them is filled up the wrath of God. And I saw as it were a sea of glass mingled with fire: and them that had gotten the victory over the beast, and over his image, and over his mark, and over the number of his name, stand on the* *sea of glass, having the harps of God. And they sing the song of Moses the servant of God, and the song of the Lamb, saying, Great and marvellous are thy works, Lord God Almighty; just and true are thy ways, thou King of saints. Who shall not fear thee, O Lord, and glorify thy name? For thou only art holy: for all nations shall come and worship before thee; for thy judgments are made manifest. And after that I looked, and, behold, the temple of the tabernacle of the testimony in heaven was opened: And the seven angels came out of the temple, having the seven plagues, clothed in pure and white linen, and having their breasts girded with golden girdles And one of the four beasts gave unto the seven angels seven golden vials full of the wrath of God, who liveth for ever and ever And the temple was filled with smoke from the glory of God, and from his power; and no man was able to enter into the temple, till the seven plagues of the seven angels were fulfilled to put them to us*

2.   **Angels bring about Instant judgement. 2 Kings 19:35**
And it came to pass that night, that the angel of the LORD went out, and smote in the camp of the Assyrians an hundred fourscore and five thousand: and when they arose early in the morning, behold, they were all dead corpses.

Isa. 37:33-36 *Therefore thus saith the LORD concerning the king of Assyria, He shall not come into this city, nor shoot an arrow there nor come before it with shields, nor cast a bank against it. By the way that he came, by the same shall he return, and shall not come into this city, saith the LORD. For I will defend this city to save it for mine own sake, and for my servant David's sake. Then the angel of the LORD went forth, and smote in the camp of the Assyrians a hundred and fourscore and five thousand: and when they arose early in the morning, behold, they were all dead corps*

3.   **An Angel is a Persecutor. Ps. 35:5-6** *Let them be as chaff before the wind: and let the angel of the LORD chase them.Psalms:35:6: Let their way be dark and slippery: and let the angel of the LORD persecute them.*

4.	**An Angel is a Deliverer. Ps. 34:2** *The angel of the LORD encampeth round about them that fear him, and delivereth them.*

5.	**An Angel is a Defender.** Num. 22:31 *Then the LORD opened the eyes of Balaam, and he saw the angel of the LORD standing in the way, and his sword drawn in his hand: and he bowed down his head, and fell flat on his face.*

6.	**An Angel gives strength. Lk. 22:43** *And there appeared an angel unto him from heaven, strengthening him.*

7.	**An Angel is a carrier of the prayers of the saints presented to God.** **Rev. 8:4** *And the smoke of the incense, which came with the prayers of the saints, ascended up before God out of the angel's hand.*

8.	**An Angel is a divine agent of preservation. Rev. 7:3-4.** *Saying, Hurt not the earth, neither the sea, nor the trees, till we have sealed the servants of our God in their foreheads. And I heard the number of them which were sealed: and there were sealed an hundred and forty and four thousand of all the tribes of the children of Israel.*
Ps. 91:11 For he shall give his angels charge over thee, to keep thee in all thy ways.

HOW DO I ENGAGE AN ANGEL?

A.	**Understand that you have power to send them on assignment.**
	Hebrew 1:13-14 *But to which of the angels said he at any time, Sit on my right hand, until I make thine enemies thy footstool? Are they not all ministering spirits, sent forth to minister for them who shall be heirs of salvation?*

B.	**Understand that they only receive command according to the word of God that you know and understand.**
	Ps.103:20 *Bless the LORD, ye his angels, that excel in strength, that do his commandments, hearkening unto the voice of his word.*

Testimony of an angelic intervention.

Billy Graham relates the following account:
Rev. John C. Paton, a missionary in the New Hebrides island, tells a terrifying story involving the protective care of angels. Hostile natives surrounded his mission headquarters, one night, intent on burning the building and killing them. John Paton and his wife prayed all through, during the terror filled night that God would deliver them.

When daylight came, they were amaze to see that the attackers had unaccountably left the premises. They thanked God for delivering them. A year later, the chief of the tribe was converted to Jesus Christ, and Mr Paton, remembering what had happened, asked the chief what had kept him and his men from burning down the house and killing them.

The chief replied in surprise, "Who were all those men you had with you there?" The missionary answered, "There were no men there, just my wife and I". The chief agreed that they had seen many men standing guard, hundreds of big men in shining garments with swords in their hands. They seemed to circle the mission station so that the natives were afraid to attack. Only then did Mr. Paton realise that God had sent his angels to protect them. The chief agreed that there was no other explanation. Could it be that God had sent His legion of Angels to protect His servants, whose lives were being endangered?.

Quotes:
1. "It is the warfare you conquer that determine your well-being in life". **- Sekudo Michael**
2. "In every battle of life, you need the finger of God at work, to run faster than your enemies" **- Sekudo Michael**

3. "In every warfare you must secure the trust of God".
   - Sekudo Michael

4. "In spiritual warfare you use your mouth and your spirit to engage God for your defence" **- Sekudo Michael**

5. "Divine judgement is the strange act of God, terminating the strange attacks of the enemy".**- Sekudo Michael**

PRAYER POINT ON: DIVINE JUDGEMENT.

1. Lord, today I send your fishers and hunters to waste the camp of the enemy and set them on fire.

2. Lord, by the hand of fishers and hunters, restore to me every stolen blessing.

3. Lord, by the mystery of the blood of Jesus, restore my lost glory.

4. Lord, today by the fire from the throne of God I decree my total deliverance from the hands of my adversaries.

5. Lord, today I launch the arrow of God against the spirit of affliction, stagnation and death sent into my family.

6. By the hand of the living God, I send the angel to slay every enemy of my destiny.

7. Lord, by the blood of Jesus, build a wall of defence around my destiny that will disappoint every arrow of the enemy.

8. Lord, today, release your angels to take over my life battles and bring my enemies to judgement.

9. Lord, every agent of darkness troubling my home, today by the hand of an angel bring them under divine judgement.

10. Lord, every manipulation that fights against the hand of God over my life, today may the fire of God consume them.

11. By the power of the blood of Jesus, I give command to the angel of God to stand between me and the forces of life contending against my destiny.

12.	Lord, by the hand of an angel bring me out from prison of life.

13.	Lord, today by the mystery of the blood of Jesus, I speak to the ground to swallow every dwelling place of the wicked. May their habitation be desolate.

14.	Lord, by the blood of Jesus, I speak to the ground of my destiny to produce its fruits.

15.	Today, I prophesy by the blood of Jesus, that my land of captivity, be turned to a land of freedom

16.	By the blood of Jesus, my life is fortified from every arrow, enchantment, divination and manipulation.

17.	Lord, every strong man standing on my land of destiny, I decree the fire of God to consume them in Jesus name.

18.	Today, by the hand of the Lord of host, I prophesy against my enemies to come under divine judgement speedily.

19.	Today, by the hand of the living God, I send a blast into the camp of the enemy for total destruction.

20.	Today by the hand of God, I send an evil spirit from the presence of God to torment my enemies to death.

21.	Today, by the power of God in the blood, I decree the strange wind of sickness, failure, disaster, stagnation, nightmare, fear, and bareness to seize forever.

22.	Today, by the blood of Jesus, I release the weapon of war directly from the throne of God against the forces of the enemy that keep the destiny of men on one spot.

23.	Today, by the blood of Jesus, I erase every negative mark of the enemy that destroys the destiny of men.

25.	Lord, by the intervention of your power, let the glory of my destiny break forth.

26.	Lord, grant me grace, and divine direction to fulfil destiny.

27.	Lord today I connect my spirit with the spirits of just men made perfect, for the release of spiritual blessings in Jesus name.

28.	Lord, let the spirit of my spiritual fathers take over my life battles and grant me victory over all my enemies.

29.	Lord, by the spirit of holy men place over my life, anoint me with fresh grace and power to know you and serve you the more.

30.	Lord, multiply your church numerically and spiritually.

31.	Lord, let your word grow mightily and prevail with testimonies following in our congregation.

WHEN GOD APPEARS, WHAT HAPPENS?

D.	**Divine Blessings. (Gen. 1:28)** *And God blessed them, and God said unto them, be fruitful, multiply and replenish the earth, and subdue it: and have dominion over the fish of the sea, and over the fowl of the air, and over every living thing that moveth upon the earth.*

The Blessing is the seal of divine pronouncement that God places on man immediately after creation.

- By creation man was born into blessing. But after he sinned, he has to pay the price to obtain the blessing. The covenant of divine blessing in the life of a man before the fall is a reality. After the fall, man has to decide whether to remain in blessing or in poverty because of the law of God in place.

- For instance, when God wants a man to reproduce or be fruitful he gave the man a seed, and the woman a womb to produce after their kind.

- The covenant of God's blessings is forever, but the blessings are not forever. Therefore, grace is required to secure the hand of God upon our lives constantly. This grace requires both spiritual and physical principles.

What is the blessing?

1. The word blessing from the original greek means to be "empowered"

Gen. 1:28 *And God blessed them, and God said unto them, Be fruitful, and multiply, and replenish the earth, and subdue it: and have dominion over the fish of the sea, and over the fowl of the air, and over every living thing that moveth upon the earth.*

2. To be blessed means to secure the hand of God over your life.
3. To be blessed means to secure generational rest.
4. To be blessed means to secure spiritual grace.
5. To be blessed means to have more than enough.
6. To be blessed means to secure the favour, kindness and goodness of God in whatsoever you do.
7. To be blessed means to be sound in your spirit soul and body.
8. To be blessed means a life of multiplication.

TYPES OF BLESSINGS

Ø **God's blessing**: If you leave where God plant you, you may not recover from wilderness experience.

Deut. 8:7-18 *For the LORD thy God bringeth thee into a good land, a land of brooks of water, of fountains and depths that spring out of valleys and hills; A land of wheat, and barley, and vines, and fig trees, and pomegranates; a land of oil olive, and honey; A land wherein thou shalt eat bread without scarceness, thou shalt not lack any thing in it; a land whose stones are iron, and out of whose hills thou mayest dig brass. When thou hast eaten and art full, then thou shalt bless the LORD thy God for the good land which he hath given thee. Beware that thou forget not the LORD thy God, in not keeping his commandments, and his judgments, and his statutes, which I command thee this day: Lest when thou hast eaten and art full, and hast built goodly houses, and dwelt therein; And when thy herds and thy flocks multiply, and thy silver and thy gold is multiplied, and all that thou hast is multiplied; Then thine heart be lifted up, and thou forget the LORD thy God, which brought thee forth out of the land of Egypt, from the house of bondage; Who led thee through that great and terrible wilderness, wherein were fiery serpents, and scorpions, and drought, where there was no water; who brought thee forth water out of the rock of flint; Who fed thee in the wilderness with manna, which thy fathers knew not, that he might humble thee, and that he might prove thee, to do thee good at thy latter end; And thou say in thine heart, My power and the might of mine hand hath gotten me this wealth. But thou shalt remember the LORD thy God: for it is he that giveth thee power to get wealth, that he may establish his covenant which he sware unto thy fathers, as it is this day. if you leave where God plant you, you may not recover from wilderness*

Ø   **Generational blessing:** Generational blessing can be acquired through spirituality.

Gen. 49:22-26 *And Laban gathered together all the men of the place, and made a feast. And it came to pass in the evening, that he took Leah his daughter, and brought her to him; and he went in unto her. And Laban gave unto his daughter Leah Zilpah his maid for an handmaid. And it came to pass, that in the morning, behold, it was Leah: and he said to Laban, What is this thou hast done unto me? did not I serve with thee for Rachel? wherefore then hast thou beguiled me? And Laban said, It must not be so done in our country, to give the younger before the firstborn.*

Num. 25:10-13. *And the LORD spake unto Moses, saying, Phinehas, the son of Eleazar, the son of Aaron the priest, hath turned my wrath away from the children of Israel, while he was zealous for my sake among them, that I consumed not the children of Israel in my jealousy. Wherefore say, Behold, I give unto him my covenant of peace: And he shall have it, and his seed after him, even the covenant of an everlasting priesthood; because he was zealous for his God, and made an atonement for the children of Israel.*

HOW TO ACHIEVE IT.

1.   **Destroy the enemy within.**

1sam 2:32 *And thou shalt see an enemy in my habitation, in all the wealth which God shall give Israel: and there shall not be an old man in thine house for ever.*

2.   **Ask God to destroy the generational force that does not make people to prosper in your family.**

2Sam.3:1 *Now there was long war between the house of Saul and the house of David: but David waxed stronger and stronger, and the house of Saul waxed weaker and weaker.*

3.   **Ask for divine showers.**

Ezekiel 34:22-31. *Therefore will I save my flock, and they shall no more be a prey; and I will judge between cattle and cattle. And I will set up one shepherd over them, and he shall feed them, even my servant David; he shall feed them, and he shall be their shepherd. And I the LORD will be their God, and my servant David a prince among them; I the LORD have spoken it. And I will make with them a covenant of peace, and will cause the evil beasts to cease out of the land: and they shall dwell safely in the wilderness, and sleep in the woods. And I will make them and the places round about my hill a blessing; and I will cause the shower to come down in his season; there shall be showers of blessing.: And the tree of the field shall yield her fruit, and the earth shall yield her increase, and they shall be safe in their land, and shall know that I am the LORD, when I have broken the bands of their yoke, and delivered them out of the hand of those that served themselves of them. And they shall no more be a prey to the heathen, neither shall the beast of the land devour them; but they shall dwell safely, and none shall make them afraid. And I will raise up for them a plant of renown, and they shall be no more consumed with hunger in the land, neither bear the shame of the heathen any more.: Thus shall they know that I the LORD their God am with them, and that they, even the house of Israel, are my people, saith the Lord GOD. And ye my flock, the flock of my pasture, are men, and I am your God, saith the Lord GOD*

4. Ask for the release of God's grace and strength to be blessed.
Deut. 15:4,7:8-11 *Save when there shall be no poor among you; for the LORD shall greatly bless thee in the land which the LORD thy God giveth thee for an inheritance to possess it: Only if thou carefully hearken unto the voice of the LORD thy God, to observe to do all these commandments which I command thee this day. For the LORD thy God blesseth thee, as he promised thee: and thou shalt lend unto many nations, but thou shalt not borrow; and thou shalt reign over many nations, but they shall not reign over thee. If there be among you a poor man of one of thy brethren within any of thy gates in thy land which the LORD thy God giveth thee, thou shalt not harden thine heart, nor shut thine hand from thy poor brother: But thou shalt open thine hand wide unto him, and shalt surely lend him sufficient for his need, in that which he wanteth. Beware that there be not a thought in thy wicked heart, saying, The seventh year, the year of release, is at hand; and thine eye be evil against thy poor brother, and thou givest him nought; and he cry unto the LORD against thee, and it be sin unto thee. Thou shalt surely give him, and thine heart shall not be grieved when thou givest unto him: because that for this thing the LORD thy God shall bless thee in all thy works, and in all that thou puttest thine hand unto. For the poor shall never cease out of the land: therefore I command thee, saying, Thou shalt open thine hand wide unto thy brother, to thy poor, and to thy needy, in thy land.*

5.   **The grace of God is the yeast in the effort of a man to produce result beyond is limit.**
Haggai 1:2-11 *Thus speaketh the LORD of hosts, saying, This people say, The time is not come, the time that the LORD's house should be built. Then came the word of the LORD by Haggai the prophet, saying, Hag:1:4: Is it time for you, O ye, to dwell in your cieled houses, and this house lie waste? Now therefore thus saith the LORD of hosts; Consider your ways. Ye have sown much, and bring in little; ye eat, but ye have not enough; ye drink, but ye are not filled with drink; ye clothe you, but there is none warm; and he that earneth wages earneth wages to put it into a bag with holes. Thus saith the LORD of hosts; Consider*

your ways. Go up to the mountain, and bring wood, and build the house; and I will take pleasure in it, and I will be glorified, saith the LORD. Ye looked for much, and, lo, it came to little; and when ye brought it home, I did blow upon it. Why? saith the LORD of hosts. Because of mine house that is waste, and ye run every man unto his own house. Therefore the heaven over you is stayed from dew, and the earth is stayed from her fruit. And I called for a drought upon the land, and upon the mountains, and upon the corn, and upon the new wine, and upon the oil, and upon that which the ground bringeth forth, and upon men, and upon cattle, and upon all the labour of the hands.

The Effect of the Blessing of God.

The blessing of God:

- Changes a man.
- Makes the man.
- Establishes the man
- Every divine blessing moves a man forward, if he abides in the covenant.

Gen. 13:1-6 *And Abram went up out of Egypt, he, and his wife, and all that he had, and Lot with him, into the south. And Abram was very rich in cattle, in silver, and in gold. And he went on his journeys from the south even to Bethel, unto the place where his tent had been at the beginning, between Bethel and Hai; Unto the place of the altar, which he had made there at the first: and there Abram called on the name of the LORD. And Lot also, which went with Abram, had flocks, and herds, and tents. And the land was not able to bear them, that they might dwell together: for their substance was great, so that they could not dwell together.*

How docs man enjoy divine blessings?

- God gives him an idea or inspiration that will change his story.
- God creates the opportunity for the idea given.
- God creates the environment (location) for the idea.

(Gen 47:14-27 *And they brought their cattle unto Joseph: and Joseph gave them bread in exchange for horses, and for the flocks, and for the cattle of the herds, and for the asses: and he fed them with bread for all their cattle for that year. When that year was ended, they came unto him the second year, and said unto him, We will not hide it from my lord, how that our money is spent; my lord also hath our herds of cattle; there is not ought left in the sight of my lord, but our bodies, and our lands: Wherefore shall we die before thine eyes, both we and our land? buy us and our land for bread, and we and our land will be servants unto Pharaoh: and give us seed, that we may live, and not die, that the land be not desolate. And Joseph bought all the land of Egypt for Pharaoh; for the Egyptians sold every man his field, because the famine prevailed over them: so the land became Pharaoh's. And as for the people, he removed them to cities from one end of the borders of Egypt even to the other end thereof. Only the land of the priests bought he not; for the priests had a portion assigned them of Pharaoh, and did eat their portion which Pharaoh gave them: wherefore they sold not their lands. Then Joseph said unto the people, Behold, I have bought you this day and your land for Pharaoh: lo, here is seed for you, and ye shall sow the land. And it shall come to pass in the increase, that ye shall give the fifth part unto Pharaoh, and four parts shall be your own, for seed of the field, and for your food, and for them of your households, and for food for your little ones. And they said, Thou hast saved our lives: let us find grace in the sight of my lord, and we will be Pharaoh's servants. And Joseph made it a law over the land of Egypt unto this day, that Pharaoh should have the fifth part; except the land of the priests only, which became not Pharaoh's. And Israel dwelt in the land of Egypt, in the country of Goshen; and they had possessions therein, and grew, and multiplied exceedingly.*
God blesses the idea (sustains).

COVENANT AVENUES FOR OBTAINING GRACE FOR DIVINE BLESSINGS.

1.   Spiritual platform

·   **The law of first fruit: To the Lord as offering.**

Ex.22:29-30 *Thou shalt not delay to offer the first of thy ripe fruits, and of thy liquors: the firstborn of thy sons shalt thou give unto me. Likewise shalt thou do with thine oxen, and with thy sheep: seven days it shall be with his dam; on the eighth day thou shalt give it me.*

Ex.20:23-19. *The first of the firstfruits of thy land thou shalt bring into the house of the LORD thy God. Thou shalt not seethe a kid in his mother's milk.*

Deut.26:1-11, *And it shall be, when thou art come in unto the land which the LORD thy God giveth thee for an inheritance, and possessest it, and dwellest therein; That thou shalt take of the first of all the fruit of the earth, which thou shalt bring of thy land that the LORD thy God giveth thee, and shalt put it in a basket, and shalt go unto the place which the LORD thy God shall choose to place his name there. And thou shalt go unto the priest that shall be in those days, and say unto him, I profess this day unto the LORD thy God, that I am come unto the country which the LORD sware unto our fathers for to give us. And the priest shall take the basket out of thine hand, and set it down before the altar of the LORD thy God. And thou shalt speak and say before the LORD thy God, A Syrian ready to perish was my father, and he went down into Egypt, and sojourned there with a few, and became there a nation, great, mighty, and populous: And the Egyptians evil entreated us, and afflicted us, and laid upon us hard bondage: And when we cried unto the LORD God of our fathers, the LORD heard our voice, and looked on our affliction, and our labour, and our oppression: And the LORD brought us forth out of Egypt with a mighty hand, and with an outstretched arm, and with great terribleness, and with signs, and with wonders: And he hath brought us into this place, and hath given us this land, even a land that floweth with milk and honey. And now, behold, I have brought the firstfruits of the land, which thou, O LORD, hast given me. And thou shalt set it before the LORD thy God, and worship before the LORD thy God: And* *thou shalt rejoice in every good thing which the LORD thy God hath given unto thee, and unto thine house, thou, and the Levite, and the stranger that is among you.*

· **The priest: As a seed of blessing.**

2kings 4:42-44 *And there came a man from Baal-shalisha, and brought the man of God bread of the firstfruits, twenty loaves of barley, and full ears of corn in the husk thereof. And he said, Give unto the people that they may eat. And his servitor said, What, should I set this before an hundred men? He said again, Give the people, that they may eat: for thus saith the LORD, They shall eat, and shall leave thereof. So he set it before them, and they did eat, and left thereof, according to the word of the LORD.*

· **The law of tithing.**

lev. 27:30-23 *And all the tithe of the land, whether of the seed of the land, or of the fruit of the tree, is the LORD's: it is holy unto the LORD. And if a man will at all redeem ought of his tithes, he shall add there to the fifth part thereof. And concerning the tithe of the herd, or of the flock, even of whatsoever passeth under the rod, the tenth shall be holy unto the LORD.*

Mal.3:7-12 *Even from the days of your fathers ye are gone away from mine ordinances, and have not kept them. Return unto me, and I will return unto you, saith the LORD of hosts. But ye said, Wherein shall we return? Will a man rob God? Yet ye have robbed me. But ye say, Wherein have we robbed thee? In tithes and offerings. Ye are cursed with a curse: for ye have robbed me, even this whole nation. Bring ye all the tithes into the storehouse, that there may be meat in mine house, and prove me now herewith, saith the LORD of hosts, if I will not open you the windows of heaven, and pour you out a blessing, that there shall not be room enough to receive it. And I will rebuke the devourer for your sakes, and he shall not destroy the fruits of your ground; neither shall your vine cast her fruit before the time in the field, saith the LORD of hosts. And all nations shall call you blessed: for ye shall be a delightsome land, saith the LORD of hosts.*

· **The law of the tabernacle.**

Haggai1:2-11 *Thus speaketh the LORD of hosts, saying, This people say, The time is not come, the time that the LORD's house should be built. Then came the word of the LORD by Haggai the prophet, saying, Is it time for you, O ye, to dwell in your cieled houses, and this house lie waste? Now therefore thus saith the LORD of hosts; Consider your ways. Ye have sown much, and bring in little; ye eat, but ye have not enough; ye drink, but ye are not filled with drink; ye clothe you, but there is none warm; and he that earneth wages earneth wages to put it into a bag with holes. Thus saith the LORD of hosts; Consider your ways. Go up to the mountain, and bring wood, and build the house; and I will take pleasure in it, and I will be glorified, saith the LORD. Ye looked for much, and, lo, it came to little; and when ye brought it home, I did blow upon it. Why? saith the LORD of hosts. Because of mine house that is waste, and ye run every man unto his own house.1:10: Therefore the heaven over you is stayed from dew, and the earth is stayed from her fruit.: And I called for a drought upon the land, and upon the mountains, and upon the corn, and upon the new wine, and upon the oil, and upon that which the ground bringeth forth, and upon men, and upon cattle, and upon all the labour of the hands.*

· **The law of faithfulness.**

Prov. 28.20 *A faithful man shall abound with blessings: but he that maketh haste to be rich shall not be innocent.*

· **The law of the poor and the needy.**

(Ps. 41:1-3) *Blessed is he that considereth the poor: the LORD will deliver him in time of trouble. The LORD will preserve him, and keep him alive; and he shall be blessed upon the earth: and thou wilt not deliver him unto the will of his enemies. The LORD will strengthen him upon the bed of languishing: thou wilt make all his bed in his sickness.*

· **The law of divine power.**

Deut 8:18 *But thou shalt remember the LORD thy God: for it is he that giveth thee power to get wealth, that he may establish his covenant which he sware unto thy fathers, as it is this day.*

· **The law of supernatural supply.**

Gen. 28:20-22. *And Jacob vowed a vow, saying, If God will be with me, and will keep me in this way that I go, and will give me bread to eat, and raiment to put on, So that I come again to my father's house in peace; then shall the LORD be my God: And this stone, which I have set for a pillar, shall be God's house: and of all that thou shalt give me I will surely give the tenth unto thee.*

· **The law of thanksgiving.**

Mal. 2:1-2 *And now, O ye priests, this commandment is for you. If ye will not hear, and if ye will not lay it to heart, to give glory unto my name, saith the LORD of hosts, I will even send a curse upon you, and I will curse your blessings: yea, I have cursed them already, because ye do not lay it to heart.*

· **They law of the "Right People".**

Gen 30:27-30 *And Laban said unto him, I pray thee, if I have found favour in thine eyes, tarry: for I have learned by experience that the LORD hath blessed me for thy sake. And he said, Appoint me thy wages, and I will give it. And he said unto him, Thou knowest how I have served thee, and how thy cattle was with me. For it was little which thou hadst before I came, and it is now increased unto a multitude; and the LORD hath blessed thee since my coming: and now when shall I provide for mine own house also?*

1Samuel 8:11-22 And he said, This will be the manner of the king that *shall reign over you: He will take your sons, and appoint them for himself, for his chariots, and to be his horsemen; and some shall run before his chariots. And he will appoint him captains over thousands, and captains over fifties; and will set them to ear his ground, and to reap his harvest, and to make his instruments of war, and instruments of his chariots. And he will take your daughters to be confectionaries, and to be cooks, and to be bakers. And he will take your fields, and your vineyards, and your oliveyards, even the best of them, and give them to his servants. And he will take the tenth of your seed, and of your vineyards, and give to his officers, and to his servants. And he will take your menservants, and your maidservants, and your goodliest young men, and your asses, and put them to his work. He will take the tenth of your sheep: and ye shall be his servants.8:18: And ye shall cry out in that day because of your king which ye shall have chosen* *you; and the LORD will not hear you in that day. Nevertheless the people refused to obey the voice of Samuel; and they said, Nay; but we will have a king over us; That we also may be like all the nations; and that our king may judge us, and go out before us, and fight our battles. And Samuel heard all the words of the people, and he rehearsed them in the ears of the LORD. And the LORD said to Samuel, Hearken unto their voice, and make them a king. And Samuel said unto the men of Israel, Go ye every man unto his city.*

2.   PHYSICAL PLATFORM

- **The law of management**: The ability to use human, material and financial resources discretionally, effectively and efficiently towards achieving maximum result in any career or business endeavour. **Prov. 2:10-11** *When wisdom entereth into thine heart, and knowledge is pleasant unto thy soul; Discretion shall preserve thee, understanding shall keep thee:*

- **The law of waste control**:   The ability to control all leakages that constitute waste or excesses to the resources of an organisation, career or business endeavour. **Prov. 18:9** *He also that is slothful in his work is brother to him that is a great waster.*

- **The law of consumption**: The ability to regulate unnecessary pleasure at the expense of the sacrifice required to move a specific organisation forward. **Prov. 21:17** *He that loveth pleasure shall be a poor man: he that loveth wine and oil shall not be rich.*

- **The Law of Liabilities**: The ability to regulate the demands of life that take more from you, and increase the asset level that will increase your in flow. **Prov.24:27** Prepare thy work *without, and make it fit for thyself in the field; and afterwards build thine house.*

- **The Law of Wisdom:** The ability to acquire currency of knowledge, training, exposure and experience relevant to one's given career, organisation and business endeavour that will help to promote smart and smooth delivery of goods and services thereby achieving higher productivity. **Prov. 16:16** *How much better is it to get wisdom than gold! and to get understanding rather to be chosen than silver!*

- **The Law of Conflict Resolution:** The ability to reconcile between motives, actions and counter actions among employees in an organisation towards promoting peaceful coexistence and character maturity, thereby achieving maximum productivity in a friendly working environment. **Prov. 16:32** *He that is slow to anger is better than the mighty; and he that ruleth his spirit than he that taketh a city.*

- **The Law of Debt:** The ability to turn any borrowed money into an investment producing profit for financial independence to avoid being a financial slave to the lender. **Prov. 22:7** *The rich ruleth over the poor, and the borrower is servant to the lender.*